Rain Forests
of the
World

Volume 4
Endangered Species–Food Web

MARSHALL CAVENDISH
NEW YORK • LONDON • TORONTO • SYDNEY

Marshall Cavendish Corporation
99 White Plains Road
Tarrytown, New York
10591-9001

Website: www.marshallcavendish.com

Consulting editors: Rolf E. Johnson, Nathan E. Kraucunas

Contributing authors: Theresa Greenaway, Jill Bailey, Michael Chinery, Malcolm Penny, Mike Linley, Philip Steele, Chris Oxlade, Ken Preston-Mafham, Rod Preston-Mafham, Clare Oliver

Discovery Books
    Managing Editor: Paul Humphrey
    Project Editor: Gianna Williams
    Text Editor: Valerie Weber
    Design Concept: Ian Winton
    Designers: Ian Winton, Keith Williams
    Cartographer: Stefan Chabluk
    Illustrators: Christian Webb, Jim Channell, Stuart Lafford

Marshall Cavendish
    Editor: Marian Armstrong
    Editorial Director: Paul Bernabeo

(cover) buttress roots in rain forest

Editor's Note: Many systems of dating have been used by different cultures throughout history. *Rain Forests of the World* uses B.C.E. (Before Common Era) and C.E. (Common Era) instead of B.C. (Before Christ) and A.D. (Anno Domini, "In the Year of Our Lord") out of respect for the diversity of the world's peoples.

The publishers would like to thank the following for their permission to reproduce photographs:
176 Werner Layer/Bruce Coleman, 177 & 178 Martin Harvey/Natural History Photographic Agency, 179 Dr. Ivan Polunin/NHPA, 180 Rod Williams/Bruce Coleman, 181 Ken Preston-Mafham/Premaphotos Wildlife, 182 David Middleton/NHPA, 183 Bruce Coleman, 184 Ken Preston-Mafham/Premaphotos Wildlife, 185 Konrad Wothe/Bruce Coleman Collection, 186 Nigel J. Dennis/NHPA, 188 Alain Compost/Bruce Coleman, 189 Gerald S. Cubitt/Bruce Coleman, 191 Paul Franklin/Oxford Scientific Films, 194 Staffan Widstrand/Bruce Coleman, 195 Nick Gordon/OSF, 196 Charles Tyler/OSF, 197 Alain Compost/Bruce Coleman, 198 John Brown/OSF, 199 Mary Evans Picture Library, 200 W. Klomp/Foto Natura/Frank Lane Pictury Agency, 202 Michael Fogden/OSF, 203 Gerald Lacz/FLPA, 204 Bruce Coleman, 205 Michael Gore/FLPA, 206 David Haring/OSF, 207 Warwick Johnson/OSF, 208 Erwin & Peggy Bauer/Bruce Coleman, 209 Gunter Ziesler/Bruce Coleman, 210 Foto Natura/FLPA, 211 Max Gibbs/OSF, 212 Linda Lewis/FLPA, 213 A. C. Parker/FLPA, 214 Daniel Heuclin/NHPA, 215 Foto Natura/FLPA, 216 M. Gunther/Foto Natura/FLPA, 217 Silvestris/FLPA, 218 Luiz Claudio Marigo/Bruce Coleman, 219 Alain Compost/Bruce Coleman, 220 Ken Preston-Mafham/Premaphotos Wildlife, 221 Foto Natura/FLPA, 222 Ken Preston-Mafham/Premaphotos Wildlife, 223 Kim Taylor/Bruce Coleman, 224 A.N.T./NHPA, 225 Christer Fredriksson/Bruce Coleman, 226 Edward Parker/OSF, 227 Alain Compost/Bruce Coleman, 228 M. Gunther/Foto Natura/FLPA, 229 Haroldo Palo Jr./NHPA, 230 Anthony Bannister/NHPA, 231 Ken Preston-Mafham/Premaphotos Wildlife, 233 Nick Gordon/OSF

The publishers would also like to thank the Friends of the Earth and WWF for permission to reproduce their logos.

Library of Congress Cataloging-in-Publication Data
Rain forests of the world.
      v. cm.
    Includes bibliographical references and index.
    Contents: v. 1. Africa-bioluminescence—v. 2. Biomass-clear-cutting—v. 3. Climate and weather-emergent — v. 4. Endangered species-food web — v. 5. Forest fire-iguana — v.6. Indonesia-manatee — v. 7. Mangrove forest-orangutan — v. 8. Orchid-red panda — v. 9. Reforestation-spider — v. 10. Squirrel-Yanomami people — v. 11. Index.
        ISBN 0-7614-7254-1 (set)
        1. Rain forests—Encyclopedias. 1. Marshall Cavendish Corporation.
    QH86 .R39 2002
    578.734—dc21

ISBN 0-7614-7254-1 (set)
ISBN 0-7614-7258-4 (vol. 4)

Printed and bound in Italy

07 06 05 04 03 02   6 5 4 3 2 1

Contents

Endangered Species

The world's rain forests are under siege, and people are the culprits. The huge belt of forest that once girdled Earth's tropical zones has already been reduced by half or even more, and the process of destruction continues daily. The rain forests are the world's most precious treasure-houses of plants and animals. Most of these cannot survive if the forest is cleared for farmland or for commercial tree plantations.

All rain forest species—from monkeys and marmosets to parrots and butterflies—depend on the very special conditions of shade and humidity found only within relatively undisturbed forest, with its almost infinite variety of microenvironments.

KEY FACTS

● Around 31 kinds of monkeys, tamarins, and marmosets in South American rain forests are endangered.

● No fewer than 44 species of parrots and macaws are endangered, mainly because people hunt them to supply the pet trade.

● The Madagascan red-and-gold skipper butterfly is known from fewer than 20 specimens.

● The golden bamboo lemur was discovered only in 1985. It is restricted to a very small area of rain forest in Madagascar.

● Clearing for oil palm plantations in Malaysia destroyed the habitat of one of the last remaining populations of the rare gaur, a relative of domestic cattle.

Every day, human activity drives at least 100 species of rain forest plants and animals to extinction. If humans continue destroying rain forests at this rate, in less than 100 years there will be no rain forests left, and only a small number of the more adaptable rain forest plants and animals will survive in the farms, plantations, and scrubby patches of forest that remain.

The World Conservation Monitoring Centre, which monitors endangered species, has established that a species is endangered when a reduction in the number of individuals of at least 50 percent has been observed in the last 10 years or is expected in the next 10 years. In deciding whether an animal is endangered, the center also considers whether the total area in which a species lives has been reduced in the last 10 years or will be lost in the next 10. A species is then considered critically endangered if the number of animals has been reduced

The gaur lives mainly in the dense forests of India and Southeast Asia. It is very susceptible to fatal diseases contracted from domestic cattle, to which it is related.

Feeding time for the orangutans at the Sepilok Rehabilitation Center on the Asian island of Borneo. Visitors flock to see these animals.

by over 80 percent in the last 10 years or if such a reduction is expected in the next 10 years, and if the species numbers fewer than 50 individuals.

Southeast Asian Forests

The rain forests of Southeast Asia are probably the richest on Earth in terms of the number of species of plants and animals that live there. The hundreds of islands that comprise the nation of Indonesia make it one of the world's richest environments for rain forest wildlife. Unfortunately the forest and its inhabitants are disappearing fast. Because many of the animals are restricted to just a single, relatively small island, they have nowhere to escape to if the trees there are felled. Extinction may then be just a few years away. Around 34 kinds of bats, for example, are endangered in Southeast Asia. Forest destruction and hunting on some of the smaller

Philippine islands has almost eliminated many rare local animals, such as the monkey-eating eagle.

Over the last 20 years huge commercial companies have destroyed vast areas of forest in Southeast Asia and replaced them with enormous

IN FOCUS

The Black or Crested Macaque

The black macaque (muh-KAK), a type of monkey, is only found in the rain forests of Sulawesi. It is one of at least seven species of macaques restricted to that fascinating island. Like most macaques, it lives in groups of 20 to 50 animals and feeds on a mixture of leaves, fruits, and small animals such as insects. Some groups are so tame that it is possible to sit within 2 ft. (60 cm) of them as they rest quietly on the ground feeding. Unfortunately this animal, which is highly prized as food, is hunted wherever it can be found.

The Sumatran rhinoceros is one of five species of rhino, all of which are endangered. There are probably fewer than 1,000 individuals left.

plantations of oil palm and rubber trees. In Borneo days-long journeys up some of the main rivers would reveal no trees within miles of the riverbanks. Everything close to the water has been felled and floated off in great rafts down to wood-processing plants.

Hundreds of species of mammals, birds, reptiles, and amphibians are now endangered in these forests; scientists can only guess at the numbers of insects and plants that are also threatened. Many of these species may have become extinct before anyone ever knew they existed.

Huge fires in the late 1990s in Borneo and Sumatra severely damaged the already endangered population of orangutans. Smoke filled the air for months, and orangutans, half blinded by the fumes, staggered out of the burning forest. Some of these refugee animals have been housed at a rehabilitation center in Sepilok in Borneo. There, animals rescued from various sources, such as clear-cut forests, zoos, or pet owners, can gradually be reintroduced to life in the wild. There is a similar rehabilitation center in Sumatra for

that country's own special subspecies of orangutan. Orangutans survive well in selectively logged forests but die out when the forest is cleared or replaced with plantations. Also, hunters often capture baby orangutans for zoos or the illegal pet trade, usually after killing the mother.

Some of the larger animals suffer more than others. At least eight species of hornbills (a bird with an enormous beak) are endangered because they need undisturbed forests with large trees to hollow out for their nests. Since almost all the larger trees are removed even in selectively logged forests, the hornbills have no nesting sites.

The Sumatran and Javan rhinoceroses are threatened both by habitat destruction and poaching for their horns. The Javan rhino is now almost confined to a single reserve on the western end of Java, where fewer than 30 specimens survive. The Sumatran rhino is much more widespread

The Central American Tapir

Tapirs (TAE-puhrs) are stout-bodied mammals with a short trunklike snout, or proboscis (pruh-BAH-sus). Only four species of tapirs occur in the world, and three of them live in the American Tropics; of these, the Central American tapir is the largest. In fact, it is the largest terrestrial mammal in the region.

The widespread destruction of the Central American forests, which has taken place with amazing speed since the 1980s, has left the tapir isolated and under threat. Most of the tapir's former home is now open grassland grazed by cattle. When properly protected, the tapir can become amazingly tame and trusting of humans.

but probably numbers under 1,000 animals. Poachers dig large pits in the forest trails used by rhinos, and thinly camouflage the pits with sticks. When a rhino ambles along, it crashes through the thin covering and falls in. Poaching for rhinos still takes place in nature reserves, where many other kinds of animals are illegally hunted for food.

Sulawesi is astoundingly rich in wildlife. Of its 127 kinds of mammals, 79 are found nowhere else. Many of these very special animals are offered openly for sale in the local meat markets. There are even restaurants where the meals contain animals illegally killed in the forests. One of the favorite meals is babirusa steaks, cut from this strange and very endangered

This poacher, caught in the act of stealing maleo eggs from an incubation mound, is helping to propel this fascinating species toward extinction.

animal that looks like a cross between a deer and a pig. Its long tusks curve up backward through the tip of its snout. It is surely doomed wherever poachers can operate unchecked.

Another popular food in Sulawesi is maleo eggs, which people prefer to chickens' eggs. The maleo lives only in Sulawesi. Its eggs are easily found because they are laid every year in the same places. If the nesting site is by the sea, the eggs are laid in black sand, which gets very hot in the sun and incubates the eggs. Inland, the warm ground near steamy volcanic vents serves the same purpose. The maleo is almost extinct in one reserve because it is near a town, and there are simply too many poachers around.

Central and South America

The rain forests of Central and South America once stretched almost intact from

southern Mexico to northern Argentina. Now the forest is broken up into fragments, some large, some small. The Amazonian rain forest, once the size of western Europe, is fast disappearing. From the air above this forest in the dry season, smoke can be seen from horizon to horizon as the forest is burned to create farmland.

The most highly prized timber trees are the mahoganies. Millions of them have been taken from the forests for making into furniture and other products that require high-quality wood. The small-leaf mahogany of the Caribbean and Central America is now very rare; the large-leaf mahogany of South America is also scarce in many areas. Sometimes even these valuable trees are burned with the rest of the forest as land is cleared for ranching.

The governments of Central and South American countries, eager to see "useless" lands developed, have encouraged people to clear rain forest land. In the 1980s the Rondônia area of Brazil, one of the world's richest wildlife areas, was chosen as a development zone for farms and ranches. Fortunately the Brazilian government made a law that farmers could only clear forest from part of their land. This means that most of the animals still survive in the patchwork of forest that remains. Many of the ranches now lie abandoned after only 20 years.

Laws to protect the valuable Atlantic Coast rain forests of eastern Brazil have come almost too late, since only about 2 percent of the forests remain. This tiny remnant is home to many highly endangered animals. The most famous of these is the golden lion tamarin, a small monkey. It has been reintroduced from captivity into a special forest reserve, where it is now doing well. Destruction of its forest home was the main cause of its decline, but thousands were also collected for the pet trade. Because of the animal's golden coat, some people are willing to pay stupendously high prices for it.

The largest South American monkey, the muriqui, is also just managing to exist in these eastern forests. Its prehensile tail can grip branches like an extra hand, aiding it as it moves around in the high canopy. Often hanging suspended by just its tail, the muriqui eats mainly fruits, seeds, and leaves.

Large groups of the equally endangered buffy-headed marmoset often accompany

The spectacular golden lion tamarin has been reintroduced into a special reserve in its native habitat, the highly threatened Atlantic Coast rain forest of Brazil.

The Madagascan red-and-gold skipper butterfly is so rare that few people have ever seen it in its rain forest home. It could easily become extinct before anyone realizes it.

the muriqui. Like most marmosets, these devote much of their time to nibbling tree trunks and feeding on the sweet sap.

Across the shady forest floor lumbers the yellow-footed tortoise. This is one of 11 species of endangered turtles and tortoises from the American Tropics or Neotropics. This large, attractive tortoise hides away during the dry season and emerges after the rains. At rest it looks like a pile of dead leaves.

Several kinds of river turtles suffer terribly from people who collect massive amounts of their eggs. The turtles lay their eggs on sandbanks along the Amazon and other major rivers. The eggs are easily found, plundered, and sold in local markets for food.

Very few rivers now house family groups of the giant otter, which used to be familiar sights. This large otter lives in holes in the banks and is an accomplished swimmer. It can become very tame and in

some protected areas will swim playfully up to a boat when called. In some places the otters share the rivers with the large Amazonian manatee. Like all manatees, these are threatened with extinction from hunting, damage to their waterweed food supplies, and collisions with boats.

African and Madagascan Forests

The rain forests of Africa have suffered less than most from destruction for commercial plantations and ranchlands. Much of the Congo's huge forest is still quite inaccessible. Strife, warfare, and disease in the region often lead to roads falling into disuse, reducing the threat to the wilderness. However, in some places, especially in western Africa, large oil palm plantations have replaced the forest. In other areas oil and logging companies have built new roads into the heart of previously untouched forest.

While selective logging and oil exploration may not directly threaten the forest and its animals, the new roads enable townspeople to go where it was previously impossible. Hunters can then satisfy the huge demand for bush meat—wild animals killed for food. Monkeys and other animals are shot in huge numbers and shipped back down the roads to markets in far-off towns.

This trade and the destruction of the forest now threaten many African animals. The most endangered of all is the drill, a type of baboon that lives deep in the forest and eats fruits, leaves, termites, and ants. It already lives in very few places in western Africa.

Easy road access also increases the threat to the more valuable trees, such as African mahoganies. Forest rangers are always on the lookout for signs of illegal pit saws: large, two-person handsaws used for turning trees into planks.

The most famous endangered species of this region is the mountain gorilla, whose habitat is confined to a small area of forest on the Uganda-Congo-Rwanda border area. Much of the forest there has been destroyed, while warfare in the region has also affected the gorillas to a certain extent. These gorillas are not safe even in reserves. This is also a dangerous area for humans, and armed guards must accompany every tourist group of gorilla watchers. Groups are normally restricted to just one hour with the animals. This minimizes disturbance, allowing the gorillas to feed in peace, and also reduces the chance of people passing on infectious diseases. The risk is so great that anyone with a cold or flu is asked to cancel or postpone his or her trip.

Madagascar has its own unique fauna and flora. Although not large, Madagascar's human population has managed to inflict a vast amount of damage on its island. At least 70 percent of the rain forests have already been destroyed and replaced by grasslands. Almost all of Madagascar's rich wildlife is in danger. The larger animals that need vast territories are most at risk because their forest habitat is broken up.

The greatest threat is to Madagascar's lemurs (LEE-muhrs). Hunting lemurs for meat is common, although in many places ancient taboos forbid harming them.

The largest of the lemurs, the indri, is threatened outside its reserves by deforestation. Extracting certain trees for making furniture deprives the indri of many leaves, fruits, and flowers that are its preferred food.

Another smaller lemur, the diademed sifaka, is at risk because it has always lived

IN FOCUS

The Spotted Owl

The U.S. Fish and Wildlife Service has listed the spotted owl as one of the endangered species of the North American rain forest. It relies upon large, undisturbed stands of the giant conifers that grow there. Logging has reduced these, thereby threatening the future of the owl by depriving it of nesting and feeding sites. Scientists are now looking at new ways of logging the forest to reduce the impact on the owl.

in rather small and spread-out groups, which reduces possibilities for breeding. It is also slow to recover any losses because each family has a new baby only every two years, unlike most other lemurs, which breed annually.

Check these out:

● Bird ● Conservation ● Deforestation ● Eagle ● Elephant ● Extinction ● Giant Otter ● Human Interference ● Madagascar ● Monkey ● Orangutan ● Tapir

Epiphyte

Epiphytes are plants that grow on other plants, especially on the trunks and branches of trees. Usually quite small, these perching plants include many ferns, thousands of different kinds of orchids, and the spiky bromeliads (broe-MEE-lee-ads). Epiphytes usually cover rain forest trees; more than half the plant species in some rain forests grow in this way.

Unlike parasites, the epiphytes use the trees merely for support and do not take any food from them, although they may compete with the trees for light and air. They are sometimes called air plants because they seem to exist purely on air, but they do need water and mineral salts just like other green plants.

KEY FACTS

● Epiphytes are often called air plants because they have no connection with the ground: they live on other plants. Sometimes they are so numerous that the trunks and branches of the supporting trees are invisible.

● Epiphytes do not directly harm the trees they grow on, but if too many of them grow on one tree, their weight may cause the branches to break.

● Several kinds of epiphytes, especially the smaller kinds of bromeliads, are grown as houseplants. Glued to pieces of rock or wood, all they need to stay alive is a little household dust and a daily squirt of water.

Water is no problem because the air is saturated with it; everything in the forest is dripping wet. Some epiphytes grow soft, water-absorbent hairs on their leaves. Orchids often sprout spongy roots that cling to the trunks and branches and

Several kinds of epiphytes are growing on this tree. The spiky one with the flower is a bromeliad.

soak up all the water they need. Most bromeliads and many ferns have cuplike leaf bases that catch and hold rain or trap water that runs down the tree trunks.

Mineral salts are also easily available, obtained mainly from the droppings of insects and other animals deposited on the branches and washed down to the epiphytes' bases. Dead leaves also accumulate around the plants and release their minerals as they rot. However, epiphytes growing on the uppermost branches have to make do with particles of dust blowing in the air for nutrients.

Epiphytes spread their seeds in several ways. Orchid seeds are small and light, blown about by the slightest breeze. Those that lodge in suitable bark crevices quickly germinate and produce new plants. The same thing happens with the dustlike spores of epiphytic ferns. Larger seeds are usually dropped by birds and monkeys; they take root in the dead leaves and other debris trapped in the forks of branches or in large cracks in the bark.

Homes for Animals

Many of the epiphytic plants in the rain forest have developed close associations with ants. Swollen stems or leaf bases provide homes for the ants, and some of the plants also secrete sugary foods for them. In return the ants protect the plants from other insects that might attempt to eat the leaves. The ants' droppings provide the plants with valuable mineral food, and some of the ants even collect the droppings of other animals and use them as fertilizer for their plant homes. Ants that make their own treetop nests from soil and chewed wood sometimes collect epiphyte seeds and plant them on the nests. The plants benefit from the ants'

IN FOCUS

Spanish Moss

Spanish moss is not a moss at all but an unusual relative of the bromeliads. It has trailing stems that hang from trees like flowing beards. The plant does not need any roots: the whole plant absorbs water. The stems are easily snapped off by the wind but continue to grow if they become anchored in a suitable spot. The stems also continue to grow when they have been gathered by birds and used to build nests. Spanish moss grows from the Amazonian rain forest northward to Florida and Georgia. People use it as a packing material and in upholstering furniture.

droppings and care, and the ants' homes are well hidden from their enemies.

Bromeliads and other epiphytes that trap water in their cup-shaped bases also provide homes for different canopy dwellers, including tree frogs, mosquitoes, flatworms, snails, salamanders, and even crabs.

Check these out:
● Ant ● Bromeliad ● Canopy
● Crustacean ● Frog and Toad

184

Erosion

Put simply, erosion is the process that wears away the rocks and soils that make up Earth's surface. Flowing water, waves, wind, and ice all erode by breaking up rocks into small fragments and moving the fragments along. In most areas, including the Tropics, rainwater flowing off the land and down streams and rivers causes most erosion.

Erosion is a natural process that has been happening for hundreds of millions of years, breaking down mountain ranges and creating valleys and canyons, shaping the surface of Earth. However, in many areas of the world, human activities have accelerated erosion, often with drastic effects on habitats and ecosystems.

There is very little natural erosion in the world's rain forests. However, when trees are cleared, the roots that hold the soil together are broken, and the fragile soil is

Devastating gully erosion in Madagascar. These hills were originally covered in dense forest.

quickly eroded away. In the worst cases it is stripped away completely, leaving a barren landscape where there was once lush forest.

Natural Erosion Protection

When heavy rain falls in a natural habitat, such as a rain forest, most raindrops hit the foliage and break into finer drops. Much of it stays on leaves or dribbles along branches, down trunks, and into the soil. The water on leaves evaporates when the sun comes out, and the water in the soil is soaked up by the plants. Hardly any water runs off or drains away through the soil unless the rain is very heavy and prolonged. Even then, the soil does not erode because it is held together by the roots of plants that grow in it. So soil normally stays where it is, supporting the growth of plants.

Soil is a mixture of particles of rock, organic material (leaf litter, dead branches, and humus), microorganisms (such as bacteria and fungi), water, and air. The organic matter helps retain water in the soil and provides nutrients (chemicals) for plants to grow.

The lush vegetation and high biodiversity of rain forests would make it appear that rain forest soil is perfect for growing crops. In fact the opposite is true: the soil is actually very poor. Although the thin top layer of the soil is rich in organic material, beneath that lies clay or sandy soil with few nutrients. The fragile nature of rain forest soil makes it extremely vulnerable to erosion.

When very heavy rain falls on soil, the raindrops dislodge bits of dirt and the

Trees at the bottom of this slope have been cleared to make space for a road. Erosion of the bare soil may wash the whole slope away.

water carries them away into streams and rivers. The steeper the ground, the faster the water runs off and the more soil it carries with it. This movement of soil is called transportation, and the moving soil is known as sediment.

Rain forests act like a reservoir, holding water and then releasing it slowly into rivers. Eroded soil cannot do this. When rain forest soils are eroded, rivers flood when it rains and run dry when it doesn't. The sediment washed downstream silts up the rivers, impeding navigation, killing wildlife, and making floods more severe.

Deforestation

When an area of rain forest is slashed and burned for growing crops, or for grazing cattle, or when it is cleared by logging, the process of erosion begins. Deforestation helps cause erosion in several ways. The foliage that protects the soil from direct heavy rain is lost. The root systems that bind the soil together are destroyed. Leaves and other plant material stop falling, which means that

IN FOCUS

The Road to Erosion

On the Malay Peninsula, a species of tree called dipterocarp dominates many areas of forest. The tree yields plenty of wood and so is popular for loggers. It is not the cutting down of the trees that directly causes erosion problems, but the extensive road building done to reach the trees and haul out the logs. The trees grow in steep-sided valleys where rains fall heavily. Rainwater flows off the roads, creating gullies. Statistics show that soil loss doubles in these logged areas.

microorganisms die and nutrients are no longer recycled.

As the organic matter disappears, the soil can no longer retain water. The shade of foliage is lost, so intense tropical sunshine reaches the soil, killing the already starving microorganisms and drying the ground to dust. Rain washes nutrients down through the soil and they are lost forever. This process, called leaching, leaves the soil useless for growing crops or for forest plants to regrow naturally.

Sheet and Gully Erosion

After deforestation, when heavy rain falls, it hits the soil hard, knocking out particles. The soil cannot soak up all the water quickly enough. On sloping ground the water flows downhill in a flat sheet, carrying soil with it. This is called sheet erosion. Any steep furrows turn into streams and quickly get larger, creating deep gullies. The gullies grow sideways and uphill, undermining any remaining vegetation. This is called gully erosion. Sheet and gully erosion eventually strip the soil away completely, leaving bare bedrock.

In an undamaged rain forest, soil loss through erosion is less than half a ton per acre (1 metric ton per hectare) per year, even on steep slopes. Where all vegetation is removed, even when crops are planted, a single tropical storm can carry 30 tons (27 metric tons) of soil from the same area. More than 200 tons (180 metric tons) can be lost in one year.

Preventing Erosion

The best way to prevent erosion where the rain forest has been cleared is to introduce better farming methods that protect the soil. This means that farmers can use the same area of land year after year without

Eucalyptus trees are planted on deforested land in Indonesia to prevent further erosion.

needing to clear more forest when the land becomes barren.

One method is to shape hillsides into terraces so that rainwater cannot flow downhill, preventing sheet and gully erosion. Another is to plant a combination of crops, some to protect the soil from rain and sunshine and some to produce food. Where erosion has occurred, soil must be bound together again to prevent more erosion. This can be achieved by planting strong grasses and fast-growing trees such as eucalyptus. Other effective methods include strip-cropping— alternating strips of crop and sod-forming crops such as hay to minimize erosion and water runoff—and growing legumes, such as clover or soybeans, to restore essential nitrogen into the soil.

IN FOCUS

Mud Slides

The effects of erosion are felt not only in the rain forest but also in and alongside the rivers into which the soil is washed. Heavy storms can wash deforested hillsides completely away in one sweep, creating lethal mud slides. In 1988 mud slides in Thailand caused by deforestation for logging and rubber plantations killed 450 people and destroyed thousands of homes. The Thai government consequently banned logging.

Check these out:
- Climate and Weather ● Deforestation
- Logging ● Reforestation ● Water

Evolution of the Rain Forest

The rain forests have survived for 100 million years, through all the climatic changes and stresses that the developing Earth could produce as it evolved from a steamy, rain-swept planet into one with the present range of global climates, from polar to equatorial. Today's rain forests are found mainly in equatorial regions, where the modern-day climate is closest to what it was like when rain forests first evolved.

Rain forests remain in three main locations. The largest of them stretches through all of Indo-china (which consists of Myanmar, Laos, Thailand, Cambodia, Vietnam, and West Malaysia), the Philippines, Indonesia, through Papua New Guinea, northern Australia, and Fiji. The next largest is in Central and South America and includes the Amazon rain forest. The third main area is in the western and central parts of Africa. There are other smaller areas, wherever enough rain falls in a warm enough climate for the forest to grow.

All these landmasses were once in the southern part of the supercontinent known as Pangaea, which broke up and drifted around the world about 100 million years ago. Botanists suggest that this was where the first flowering plants evolved and thus where the first rain forests stood. Pieces of the southern part, Gondwana, drifted apart to form Africa, South America, Australia, the Indian peninsula, and Antarctica.

KEY FACTS

● **The tropical rain forests we recognize today were formed 100 million years ago during the Cretaceous period, when the first flowering plants evolved.**

● **Fossil evidence shows that rain forests most likely appeared first on the ancient supercontinent of Gondwana.**

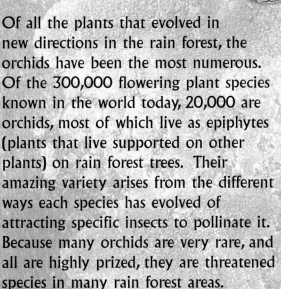

IN FOCUS

A Myriad of Orchids

Of all the plants that evolved in new directions in the rain forest, the orchids have been the most numerous. Of the 300,000 flowering plant species known in the world today, 20,000 are orchids, most of which live as epiphytes (plants that live supported on other plants) on rain forest trees. Their amazing variety arises from the different ways each species has evolved of attracting specific insects to pollinate it. Because many orchids are very rare, and all are highly prized, they are threatened species in many rain forest areas.

When these pieces arrived at their current positions, each section of the original supercontinent was affected by local conditions to evolve in a slightly different way. Most notable was Madagascar, isolated from Africa for millions of years, where plants such as the bottle palm and animals such as the lemurs (LEE-muhrs), found nowhere else in the world, were able to evolve and survive.

Evolution and Flowering Plants

As Gondwana was dispersed around the world, each piece of it carried the telltale plants that held the secret of the dawn of rain forest history. Fossil plants show that about 100 million years ago, during the Cretaceous period, the climate of the whole planet was warm and damp. It was in this climate that flowering plants first evolved. The advantage of having flowers was that they could attract animals such as insects and birds to carry pollen from one flower to another and disperse seeds, instead of having to rely on the wind to do it.

The ways in which the first flowers attracted animals to carry their pollen varied. Some flowers were brightly colored, showing insects where the center of the flower was and drawing them in to collect pollen as food. Others produced enticing scents for the same purpose. Still others began to produce nectar, which insects and birds came to eat. Pollen grains that brushed off on the visitors were carried to the next flower they fed on.

Flowering plants soon covered much of the land surface in dense stands—the first rain forests. These forests were not identical to the tropical rain forests of today because they contained very different plants. However, the structure of the plant community must have looked very similar—tall, slender, densely packed trees towering above a dark, damp forest floor.

There are 13 families of primitive flowering plants, all treelike, and all but two of them found almost exclusively in the Tropics. Three live mainly in the rain forests of the Northern Hemisphere, and five in tropical Australia and New Guinea. One family is found in both Australasia and South America, and others grow in both South America and western Africa. Fossils of the South American families

CONTINENTAL DRIFT

About 250 million years ago, Earth's land surface was dominated by a single supercontinent known as Pangaea. The land of the southern part of Pangaea is known as Gondwana. Rain forests dominated by ferns covered the earth's surface.

About 100 million years ago, the plates of Earth's crust began to drift apart, and Pangaea began to break up. Africa, South America, Australia, Antarctica, and India began to split off from Gondwana. The climate was warm and damp, and rain forests covered most of the land surface. Flowering plants began to evolve.

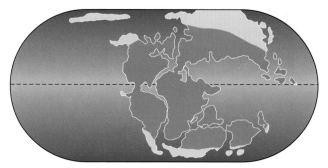

have been found in Antarctica, which was once just as warm as the rest of the world.

Climate Changes

About 40 million years ago the world's climate became cooler and drier. Less water evaporated from the surface of the oceans, so there were fewer clouds and therefore less rain. The forests that once covered the majority of Earth's land surface were restricted to only the places that were still warm and damp; in other words, to the Tropics around the equator. Even there, they could not grow everywhere: they were limited to the coastal regions, where cool winds from the sea formed rain clouds over the land; and to highlands, where rising air currents formed clouds over the hills to supply rain year-round.

In places where not enough rain fell to support a rain forest, the plants had to adapt to living in a different way, with less water and a drier atmosphere. The deciduous forests of the Tropics developed from these ecosystems, becoming the plant life of the deserts and temperate zones. Some plants became adapted to living on mountains, some in swamps, and some in pools and rivers. Others even colonized the high arctic tundra. Over millions of years, plants

Ferns Forever

Although the flowering plants quickly became the dominant form in the rain forests, the much more ancient line of ferns, which reproduce with spores, not seeds, did not die out. They continued to evolve along their own lines, and the rain forest is today the home of a great variety of this ancient but still highly successful type of plant.

Sixty-five million years ago, the continents were almost in their present-day positions. Then, about 40 million years ago, the earth's climate began to turn drier.

Tropical rain forests retreated, growing only in damp places close to the equator. Today tropical rain forests are limited to a few equatorial regions.

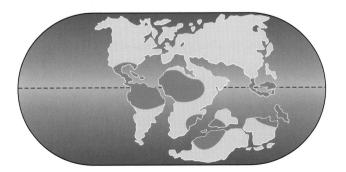

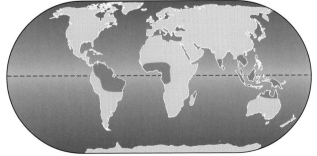

evolved to make use of almost every habitat on Earth. In all, there are now estimated to be more than 300,000 species of flowering plants, all descended from the original rain forest plants as a result of the series of changes in the climate and landscape.

About 1.5 million years ago, a long succession of ice ages began, and the world's climate began to change again. Long, cold, dry periods resulted when the ice caps advanced from the poles. These periods were interspersed with wetter, warmer times when the ice caps retreated again. All the world's plant communities were under great stress during this period, and the rain forests became the smallest they have ever been.

Some survived only in small refuges, perhaps on islands, in deep valleys, or high on hills where enough rain still fell to keep them going. Some of these refuges can still be identified, especially in the Amazon River basin, because of the number and variety of ancient species that survive there. The last ice age ended about 10,000 years ago, so the present distribution of rain forests can be said to date from then.

Evolution of Animal Life

Life in the rain forests was able to evolve into many successful forms. The enormous variety of plants offered a vast range of evolutionary possibilities for animals. Insects evolved to match the

PREHISTORIC RAIN FORESTS

192

kaleidoscopic variety of flowers; and later, animals evolved to feed on the insects. For plant-eating animals, the rain forest offered an almost infinite menu of leaves, flowers, fruits, and seeds. The different levels (strata) in the trees provided an enormous number of ecological niches, to which birds and monkeys, moths and spiders could become adapted.

Today's Rain Forests

Today's rain forests contain not only representatives of the oldest flowering plants on Earth, but also the greatest variety of modern plants. The competition for resources such as water and light and for pollinators—which may range from tiny insects to bats and large birds—has ensured that countless possible shapes and ways of life have been endured by rain forest plants in their long evolutionary history.

Another important factor of rain forest evolution is that in Africa lies the home of what are believed to be the closest relations of humans—chimpanzees and gorillas. Chimps share 98 percent of their genes with humans, and they evolved in the ancient forests. Some scientists therefore think of these forests as our ancestral home.

Check these out:
- Climate and Weather ● Fern
- Flowering Plant ● Orchid ● Pollination
- Rain Forest

Dinosaurs flourished between 230 million and 65 million years ago. The climate of the earth was warm and damp, and rain forests covered most of the earth's surface.

Exploitation

The term *exploit* has two meanings. The first is "to make use of a valuable resource." The second is "to use selfishly for one's own ends." When it comes to rain forest exploitation, these two meanings often overlap.

Humans have always exploited the rain forest for its resources. However, while peoples who live in the rain forests have historically cared for this valuable resource, incomers have begun the destruction of rain forests in an act of selfishness. Because of incomers' exploitation of rain forest resources, future generations will be unable to gain from many benefits that the forests may yet have to offer.

KEY FACTS

● It has been estimated that any area of Amazon rain forest can produce six times more profit from careful harvesting of natural produce than from logging.

● About 7,000 medicines currently in use originated from plants, many of them from rain forest sources.

● The Kayapo people of Brazil launched a successful international campaign against building large dams in their homeland.

Plants and Trees

The primary resources being exploited come from the rain forest itself—from the trees and other plants, from their bark, roots, fruits, leaves, and seeds. People living in forests have always used wood for fuel and making shelters. They rarely use up large amounts of timber, but where forests border farming villages or larger settlements, inhabitants may clear large areas of forest for fuel. Villagers may also burn wood to manufacture charcoal for sale.

Large-scale damage to rain forests begins when companies start to use the forest for timber and the logging industry moves in. Tropical hardwoods, such as teak and mahogany, are the most durable and resistant to rot and so are the most valuable. However, they come from the slowest-growing trees, whose removal from the forest causes long-term disruption to the environment. By exploiting tropical forests, many of the world's poorer nations can bring in much-needed wealth. A single teak log can be worth $20,000. Tropical old-growth hardwoods make up 15 percent of all international trade in

A tree trunk is trimmed in Manú National Park in Peru. It was felled without permission. Illegal logging is devastating many protected regions.

A Piaroa man, carrying a blowgun for hunting, checks his village's forest gardens in Venezuela. Such clearings are less harmful than large-scale plantations.

timber. Major exporters include India, Indonesia, Malaysia, the Philippines, Brazil, and Nigeria.

However, logging is a major environmental problem and one of the chief causes of deforestation. Logging may create many secondary problems, too. Roads built to transport timber open the forest up to settlement and to other forms of exploitation.

Minerals and Water
Rain forest vegetation may cover land that contains valuable mineral resources such as copper. Mineral traces washed down forest streams may encourage fortune hunters to pan for gold. Other natural resources of the forest may then be destroyed to exploit the mineral

wealth. Mining scars the landscape, pollutes rivers, destroys forests, and brings in roads.

The rain that falls on the forest is a major resource in itself. It drains into large, strong-flowing rivers that can be harnessed to generate electricity for cities and industrial development. However, hydroelectric projects include dams, which are expensive to build, disrupt forest life, and flood large areas.

Soil for Farming
Land-hungry farmers see rain forest soil as a valuable resource. Native peoples have always cleared patches of forest by the slash-and-burn method, moving on when the land needed to recover. However, huge areas of the Amazon rain forest have now been felled or burned for commercial farming and cattle ranching. Rain forest land is suited for supporting a rain forest, not for farming. Soon after the trees are cleared away, the nutrients in the soil are exhausted. The soil, no longer held together by tree roots, is washed away by

IN FOCUS

Iroko: A Tropical Hardwood

The iroko is a large rain forest tree that grows in western African countries such as the Ivory Coast and Ghana. It has a density of about 40 lb. per cubic foot (660 kg per cubic meter), which makes it a hardwood. Since the 1940s it has been widely felled as a cheap substitute for teak. Its hardness makes it resistant to pest damage and weathering, so it is widely used for making yard furniture, decks, and other items in the home. Responding to growing concern about the disappearance of the rain forests, most suppliers now specify that their iroko comes from sustainable forests.

tropical rains. Land cleared in this way has little chance of recovering and becoming primary forest once more.

Other Forest Products

There are ways of exploiting rain forest resources that are less destructive. Humans take more than just timber from rain forest trees. They tap rubber trees for a sticky, milky juice called latex, which is processed into natural rubber in a factory. Most natural rubber today is collected from plantations rather than wild plants. Rain forest trees may yet be found to provide all sorts of other useful products—natural insecticides, for example, or fibers from bark.

Brazil nuts, used in candies and desserts and also as an ingredient in shampoo and soap, need to grow in the rain forest so that they can be pollinated by the bees living there. If valuable products like these nuts can be grown or gathered within the natural forest, then the forest can be saved from destruction and remain commercially productive at the

This elderly Iban man is tapping natural rubber from trees in Sarawak, in the hilly interior of northwestern Borneo.

same time. This means that indigenous people can earn an income that enables them to stay in the forest. For example, Brazil's Kayapo people now profit from making Brazil-nut oil. In Africa, beekeeping for honey has been tried as another way of earning income from the forest without inflicting damage on the environment.

Rain Forest Medicines

The rain forests have always provided the peoples who live there with herbal remedies and medicines. Many of these plants are now used to make medical cures that have saved lives or eased pain around the world; approximately 40 percent of all medicines in use today are

IN FOCUS

The Medicine Cabinet

A chemical taken from the bark of lianas (climbing plants of the South American forests) is used to treat patients with diseases of the nervous system called multiple sclerosis and Parkinson's disease. Plant substances extracted from the rosy periwinkle, a plant native to Madagascar, are used for treating Hodgkin's disease, a form of cancer. Quinine, used to treat malaria, comes from the bark of the South American cinchona tree.

derived from plants and animals, especially those found in the rain forests. Some medicines use actual extracts of bark, roots, leaves, and so on. Others simply copy the chemical structures of rain forest extracts to create synthetic (human-made) versions of the active ingredient.

The rain forest may yet hold the key to curing major illnesses. To increase the odds of finding useful drugs, researchers are exploring the medical practices of native healers, whose traditional use of plants gives clues about which species may be beneficial for curing specific illnesses. This kind of rain forest exploitation is good for humanity and good for the forest.

Wildlife as a Resource

Secondary rain forest resources are many. The animals and birds of the forest are hunted for food, skins, horns, or ivory, or for sale to collectors. Again, international treaties now ban the trade in endangered species and related products, but illegal hunting and trading are widespread in all rain forest regions. Controlled breeding of animals such as crocodiles for their skins or establishing butterfly farms may reduce the pressure on wild populations. Conservation of wild creatures is the only way to ensure biodiversity.

Making a Difference

Our world is wasteful of resources, even when they have been obtained with great difficulty and expense. Instead, objects should be built to last, and materials should be recycled wherever possible.

Economic changes could be introduced that make poorer countries less dependent on timber or minerals as resources. Removing or reducing the heavy burden of international debt that any single country has to repay would lessen their need to exploit rain forest resources. Pharmaceutical companies that discover and develop rain forest–based cures should be prepared to donate a percentage of their profits to benefit the countries where the plants were discovered.

The challenge is to make the best use of the rain forest as a precious resource without destroying it in the process.

Check these out:
- Biotechnology
- Cattle Ranching
- Clear-Cutting
- Conservation
- Deforestation
- Forestry
- Kayapo People
- Logging
- Medicinal Plant
- Mining
- Oil Exploration
- Poaching

A Dyak woman collects plants for use in medicines in East Kalimantan, Borneo.

For thousands of years, only the peoples who hunted and gathered food in the rain forests knew their secrets. Even people who farmed land around the fringes of the forests feared entering this shadowy green world.

Travelers mostly avoided the world's rain forests, too. In Africa they heard strange rumors of small forest people and of gigantic apes. In the Americas there was talk of fierce headhunters and man-eating snakes. Many travelers' tales were exaggerated or simply untrue. Instead, forest exploration posed other challenges.

KEY FACTS

● Only 200 years ago, maps of central Africa were still blank.

● One way modern scientists have devised of examining the rain forest canopy is to lower a platform to the trees from a dirigible or airship.

● Rain forest research has already yielded medical treatments for hypertension, Hodgkin's disease, and rheumatoid arthritis.

Secret Worlds

There are many reasons why the world's rain forests remained a barrier to systematic human exploration for so long. The vegetation is dense; people have to hack through it with heavy knives to make pathways. There are few lookout points or landmarks. In the past there were no roads and few tracks. Travel was often easiest by river.

A head for heights is a help when it comes to rain forest research. Here, an international research team explores the canopy of a Panamanian forest.

IN FOCUS

An Early Pioneer

Henry Morton Stanley (1841–1904) was a Welsh-born American journalist. In 1874 he set out from East Africa for the Lualaba, the western headstream of the Congo River. He went on to follow the course of the Congo all the way to the Atlantic Ocean.

The climate is hot, humid, and wet, so it is hard to preserve food or keep equipment dry and in good repair. Fierce ants and stinging insects, snakes, and crocodiles pose constant threats. To an outsider the environment seems hostile and exhausting.

Early Exploration

Systematic exploration of the world's rain forest zones began only in the late 1700s. The reasons outsiders first ventured into these remote regions are varied. Some explorers were scientists or geographers trying to find out more about natural history, landscape features, or local peoples. Some were archaeologists searching for the ruined cities of lost civilizations. Others were in the service of politicians and governments trying to gain control of new territories or colonies. Some were traders and merchants in search of rubber or other valuable resources. There were farmers in search of land for plantations, and loggers, and mining prospectors in search of wealth. Churches sent missionaries to convert rain forest peoples.

The early explorers risked their lives. Some died of tropical diseases and parasites, some from attack by hostile groups. However, many of them performed valuable work.

With the invention of the airplane in the 20th century, rain forest exploration was revolutionized. People could then travel above the forest canopy and trace the course of rivers from the air. In 1933 an American pilot named Jimmy Angel was flying over the highlands of southern Venezuela in search of gold. Amid the dense tropical forests and rocky cliffs below he first saw the spectacular site of the world's highest waterfall, Cherún-Merú, or Angel Falls.

On the Ground

Why do people explore the rain forest today? After all, even the most remote regions can now be mapped from space by satellites. Why does ground-level exploration still take place?

Today's explorers are mainly scientists interested in finding out more about rain forests, recording plant and animal species and finding out how they relate to each other. They may be looking for new

Research scientists compare notes after a hard day's work. They have returned to a rain forest base camp near Tresor, Kaw, in French Guiana.

medical cures in forest trees or herbs, or they may be trying to estimate the size of an endangered wildlife population. They may be studying damage done to areas of forest by illegal logging or hunting, or they may be restoring affected ecosystems.

Planning to Explore

Modern rain forest expeditions need as much careful planning as they did in the early days, although now explorers have radio contact and can use airplanes to drop supplies or perform rescues. Inflatable boats with high-powered motors are practical for river travel, although canoes or small boats are still useful. Powerful four-wheel-drive vehicles are often used when roads do exist through

the forest, for tropical rains can turn unsurfaced roads and tracks into swamps.

Rain forest exploration today is often vertical as well as horizontal. Ropes and climbing equipment may be taken to explore the high levels of trees, all the way up to the forest canopy. The lines are shot over the upper branches using crossbows. For long-term projects, rope walkways and platforms are constructed at canopy level. In more accessible areas, tall construction cranes have even been used with some success.

The high humidity of the climate, combined with the hard trekking through dense forest, makes humans sweat large amounts of water and salt, and both of these need replacing. Expedition members may need to drink nearly 6 quarts (5.7 liters) of water a day and swallow salt tablets.

Rain forest explorers or members of scientific expeditions must take mosquito nets and medicine for malaria and other tropical diseases that mosquitoes and other insects may carry. Bloodsucking leeches often stick to the body; they are very difficult to remove. Snakebites, bee stings, and ant or spider bites are all possible hazards. Explorers normally sleep in hammocks rather than on the ground to stay clear of trouble from creeping creatures.

Research scientists take all kinds of specialized equipment into the forest. They may bring long cutting poles, lamps for attracting moths and other flying insects, sieves and funnels for sifting through leaf litter, nets for trapping birds or other animals, cameras, tape recorders, and laptop computers.

Figuring Out the Big Picture

Rain forest research may be sponsored by nongovernment organizations (NGOs) or by governments. For example, the United Kingdom–based Fauna and Flora Preservation Society (FFPS) has researched the conservation of gorillas in Rwanda. New York–based Wildlife Conservation International has studied forest elephants in Africa and monkeys in Borneo. The Malayan Nature Society and the Nigerian Conservation Foundation have done the work necessary to establish national parks. The World Wide Fund for Nature (WWF) is one of the leading NGOs working for tropical rain forest conservation, having been in the field since 1962. This organization has

explored and surveyed rain forest ecosystems from China to Costa Rica. Friends of the Earth (FoE) monitors the international timber trade, researching the effects of logging on rain forest species.

The results of individual research projects are usually exchanged and evaluated internationally. Bodies such as the World Conservation Union (IUCN) collect data from many different organizations and put together the big picture. Members of the IUCN include both governments and NGOs. Since 1985 rain forest research has been coordinated by the Tropical Forestry Action Plan, set up by the World Forestry Congress held in Mexico City in that year. Evaluation of all the research allows scientists to determine—and possibly protect—the fate of rain forest species.

Check these out:
- **Biomass** ● **Biotechnology**
- **Canopy** ● **Careers** ● **Conservation**
- **Medicinal Plant**

Australian Research

IN FOCUS

The Tropical Forest Research Centre in Queensland, Australia, is a research base for scientists studying rain forest ecology. By painstakingly recording forest species one by one, they have put together an overall picture of regional biodiversity. They have already established that although tropical rain forests cover only 0.1 percent of Australia's landmass, they contain 30 percent of all Australia's marsupials (pouched mammals), 60 percent of its bats, 30 percent of its frogs, 62 percent of its butterflies, 23 percent of its reptiles, 18 percent of its birds, and 25 percent of all plant genera (groups).

Extinction

Extinction occurs when an entire species of plant or animal dies out forever. Extinction can be a natural process, an essential part of evolution, of the cycle of life and death. The most common natural cause of extinction is a change in climate, which usually happens very slowly over many thousands of years. However, since humans appeared, hunting, destruction of habitat, and the introduction of new species to places where they have never lived before have caused the extinction of species all over the world. These events happen so fast that the animals do not have time to evolve with characteristics that would help them cope with the changes. Thus they die out.

KEY FACTS

● Today, plants and animals are becoming extinct faster than ever before, mainly because humans are destroying their habitat.

● Bird species are becoming extinct today 30,000 times faster than dinosaur species were during prehistoric times.

Extinction has gone on since life on Earth began. Sometimes it was very quick, involving many species. At the end of the Cretaceous period, 65 million years ago, the dinosaurs died out, probably because of a sudden change in the climate, which may have been caused by a giant meteorite hitting Earth. Many other species of plants and animals also vanished at that time. It is believed that prior to this mass extinction, dinosaurs became extinct at the rate of about one species every 1,000 years. Today's rates of extinction are much higher.

Decreasing Life Expectancy

Scientists studying birds have determined that most species survive for about 40,000 years before becoming extinct naturally. Today, this "species life

This tank bromeliad, once found in southeastern Brazil, is extinct in the wild. This specimen is growing in a greenhouse.

expectancy" has fallen to 16,000 years. More than half the birds that have become extinct since the mid-19th century, many of them rain forest species, died out because of humans hunting them or destroying their habitat.

Between 5,000 and 10,000 new species of plants and animals are recognized every year, out of a total of about 1.6 million named species in the world. Many millions of species have not yet been discovered; the total number of species in the world must be more than 3 million and possibly as many as 10 million.

One careful estimate shows that about 1 million species became extinct between 1975 and 2000. That works out to 100 species per day, or one every 15 minutes. Many of them, especially fungi, insects, and small snails, for example, died out before we even knew they existed.

The total rate of deforestation is difficult to estimate, but if rain forest is being destroyed at the rate of about 77,000 square miles (200,000 km²) a year, which may be a low estimate, we shall lose about 30 species of birds every year. This is 30,000 times faster than the extinction rate of the dinosaurs.

Some creatures become extinct quicker than others. Birds are dying out twice as fast as mammals, and fish six times as quickly. Seventy plants become extinct for every mammal, and no less than 180 species of insects. Scientists estimate that the destruction of the world's tropical rain forests is driving as many as 27,000 species annually —three species per hour—into extinction.

The main reason for this rate of extinction is the growth rate of the human population and its need for food. The world population reached 6 billion in 1999 and shows no sign of slowing down. Because they are losing their habitat so quickly, the only hope for some rare species is to be bred in captivity until enough suitable and safe habitat has been established for them to be released once more into the wild.

Check these out:
- Bird
- Central America
- Deforestation
- Endangered Species
- Human Interference
- Parrot, Macaw, and Parakeet

IN FOCUS

Parrots in Danger

Eight species of large parrots have become extinct in the last 400 or 500 years, partly from humans destroying their habitat, partly from hunters capturing them for the pet trade or to use their bright plumage. Today the Puerto Rican parrot (shown below) has a population of less than 100 and might be on the way to joining the others.

Feeding

Animals eat plants, other animals, or the remains of living things. There are no marked seasons in many rain forests, and plants can be found in flower and fruit all year round. This makes it possible for animals to specialize in eating only certain foods without risking starvation.

The Leaf Eaters

An incredible variety of animals feed on plants, from tiny sap-sucking bugs to deer, tapirs (TAE-puhrs), monkeys, and huge forest elephants. Plant eaters, or herbivores, may not have to search far to find a meal, but they often have to feed for many hours each day to obtain the nutrients they need.

Plants present a particular digestive challenge because of the tough fibers in their cell walls. Cellulose fibers are insoluble, and most animals cannot digest them. Caterpillars, grasshoppers, and katydids have sharp, saw-edged jaws for cutting leaves. Mammals that feed on leaves have big molars—large teeth with ridges— at the back of the jaw for grinding up the plant tissues. The front teeth, or incisors, are sharp for cutting off leaves.

With a clear view of the canopy, a squirrel monkey's excellent color vision helps it spot nectar-rich flowers and juicy fruits.

204

A few animals, such as deer and okapis, have a space between the front teeth and the back teeth called the diastema (die-uh-STEE-muh). This space allows the tongue to mix food with saliva to start digestion. The teeth of many leaf eaters grow throughout the animal's life to make up for being worn down by the constant grinding.

Leaf eaters have special chambers in their stomachs that are full of bacteria for digesting cellulose. After time in the bacteria chamber, where it is broken down and softened, the food, called cud, is returned to the mouth for more chewing. It is then swallowed for good. Even ordinary herbivores have extra-long intestines to allow plenty of area for nutrient absorption.

Liquid Feeders

Animals that feed on plant sap or nectar need a way to suck up the sugary liquid. Sap-sucking bugs have tube-shaped, sucking mouthparts enclosed inside other mouthparts, which are pointed and sharp for cutting into the plant to reach the sap.

Nectar feeders such as bees, butterflies, and moths also have tubelike mouthparts. Butterflies and

An Australian honeyeater inserts its slender bill into a tube-shaped flower to sip nectar.

moths can roll these up out of the way when not feeding.

The long, slender bills of nectar-feeding hummingbirds and sunbirds reach the nectaries deep inside flowers. Hummingbirds' tongues roll up lengthwise at the tip to form a sucking tube. The honey possum of Australia, which feeds almost exclusively on nectar, has a similar tongue.

Fruit, Nut, and Seed Eaters

Hard coats cover nuts and seeds. Birds that feed on seeds, such as finches and barbets, usually have large, powerful beaks to break these coats. Parrots and macaws use the sharp points of their hooked bills to bore into tough fruits, holding them firmly in their claws, which have two forward-facing toes and two backward-facing toes.

IN FOCUS

A Silken Shroud

A spider does not need to chew its prey. When it pounces on an insect or catches one in its web, it delivers a poisonous bite to paralyze it. Then it wraps the prey in silk to make sure it cannot move—spiders too are vulnerable to insect bites and stings. The spider then injects this insect parcel with digestive fluids and waits for the fluids to work. When the prey has been reduced to a tasty soup, the spider sucks it up.

Birds have no teeth to chew food. Before food passes into their stomachs, it enters a chamber called the crop, where powerful muscles help break it down. Birds often swallow small stones and grit to help grind plant material.

Rodents and marsupials are nut specialists. Long, sharp, curving front teeth (incisors) cut into the nut, and powerful jaw muscles help them bite hard enough to crack the shell. One of the world's largest rodents, the agouti (uh-GOO-tee) of Central and South American rain forests, can even tackle huge Brazil nuts weighing several pounds.

Blood Suckers

Vampire bats, which feed on the blood of large mammals, including cattle and horses, have teeth so sharp that their victims are usually unaware they have been bitten. The bats lap up the blood with their tongues.

Leeches have suckerlike mouths with sharp jaws that make a Y-shaped incision. As they bite, they inject an anesthetic to numb the area and a substance to prevent clotting. As they suck up the blood, their bodies swell.

Meat Eaters

Meat-eating mammals have very distinctive teeth. The front teeth (incisors) are sharp for cutting off pieces of flesh. Just behind them grow long, pointed teeth (canines), sometimes called fangs, for piercing and holding the prey. Jagged, pointed teeth (carnassials) follow, acting like scissors to shear the flesh. Finally the back teeth, or molars, have pointed cusps to help crush and chew the flesh.

Snakes have long pointed fangs for gripping their prey. Some inject poison to paralyze their victim, while others coil around the prey to suffocate it. Some lizards' sharp pointed teeth can crush insects and other small animals. Crocodiles and caimans have large numbers of pointed teeth that interlock to grip struggling prey.

Birds of prey often have a curved bill with a pointed hook at the end for tearing into flesh. Armed with beaks like

IN FOCUS

Nimble Fingers

The aye-aye (IE-ie) of Madagascar hunts for insect larvae at night. It relies on its huge, furless ears to pick up the sounds of insect grubs moving under the bark of decaying trees. It will tap the surface with its long middle finger to see if something moves. When it finds a grub, the aye-aye uses its powerful front teeth to bite through the wood, then scoops out the grub with its extremely long third finger. This finger is much longer and thinner than the other fingers and can easily reach into crevices in the wood. The aye-aye uses a similar tactic to pierce egg shells (below) before sucking out the contents.

206

this, eagles, hawks, and owls also use their sharp, curved talons to hold the carcass down while they feed. Some birds, such as herons, darters, and shrikes, have sharp, pointed bills for spearing their prey. Woodpeckers hammer holes in rotting wood to get at insect grubs. Scythebills use a gentler tactic: their long, slender, curving bills fish insects out of crevices in bark.

Hunting Insects

Predatory (hunting) insects, crustaceans, and other small invertebrates—such as praying mantids, army ants, and centipedes—rely on cutting and even sawlike mouthparts. Like the rest of their bodies, the mouthparts of insects are covered in a tough outer coat made of an extremely hard substance called chitin.

Chitin (KIE-ten) poses a problem for animals that eat insects. Insect eaters such as bats, shrews, tenrecs, and moon rats (a kind of hedgehog) have lots of small, pointed teeth to pierce and crush the tough coats or shells of their insect prey. Insect-eating birds have pointed beaks to stab their prey. Caterpillars and other grubs provide a softer meal; birds that eat these may have quite slender bills.

Frogs and toads have surprisingly long, sticky tongues. They lie in wait for passing insects, then shoot out their tongue at an amazing speed to catch them. The chameleon (kuh-MEEL-yuhn) stalks its prey incredibly slowly until it gets close enough to shoot out its sticky tongue, which may be longer than its body.

Ant-eating animals, such as armadillos, anteaters, pangolins, and numbats, face a special challenge—the bites and stings of their prey. Protective scales cover armadillos' and pangolins' bodies, while extra-tough skin covers the bare snouts of

A chameleon swallows a grasshopper. Its eyes can move independently, so it can spot an insect anywhere around it.

anteaters like the tamandua and kinkajou. All these animals use their long tongues coated with sticky saliva to reach deep into ant and termite nests to fish for their supper. Long, powerful, curving front claws help them tear open the nests.

Check these out:
- Carnivore
- Food
- Food Web
- Herbivore
- Insectivore

207

Ferns are primitive plants that have been around for millions of years. The dinosaurs of the Cretaceous period probably feasted on ferns.

Large fern leaves, called fronds, often divide again and again into smaller leaflets. Some ferns sport long, ribbonlike leaves, and a few have upright spoon-shaped fronds. Tufts of fern fronds sprout from trailing underground stems called rhizomes (RIE-zoems).

Instead of seeds, ferns produce tiny dustlike spores that drift on the wind to distant areas. They are often some of the first plants to colonize areas of forest that have been cleared for cultivation. In some areas tree ferns become so numerous that they form their own forests.

Trapping Light, Food, and Water

Ferns of the shady forest floor are often very big, with a large surface area for trapping what little light reaches them. Out in the open, away from the shade, ferns must avoid drying out. Star-shaped hairs that trap a layer of moist air next to the leaf cover the fronds of felt ferns; the leaf itself can also curl up to avoid losing water. Some polypody ferns have natural lines of weakness on the stalks of their fronds. In dry conditions these give way, and the frond is shed, thus reducing their need for water.

Other ferns store food and water in their rhizomes. These then become targets for thirsty and hungry animals, so they are often protected by sharp spines.

Staghorn ferns are unusual in that their main fronds are huge and shieldlike, while the spore-bearing fronds are quite different. They are narrower, like branching straps.

Hanging Gardens

Bracket ferns live high on the branches of forest trees. The dead remains of their lower leaves form a basket that traps other leaves. These rot down into a natural compost, and the fern sends roots into it to feed. Other plants soon move in—ribbon ferns, orchids, and other flowers. Ants make their nests there, adding to the compost of this natural hanging garden, which soon trails down below the branch.

The High Life

Many ferns live on the branches and trunks of forest trees, some high in the canopy. Tiny cracks in the bark allow the ferns to take hold. Rainwater and fog droplets trickling down the bark dissolve nutrients that the ferns absorb.

Hare's foot ferns have trailing fronds over 3 feet (1 m) long that dangle from branches like glossy green curtains. Dangling adder's-tongue and ribbon ferns resemble green ribbons. Bird's-nest and staghorn ferns have highly branched, wiry roots that protect more delicate roots from damage and also hold water like a sponge.

Many of these ferns actually start life on the forest floor. They creep over the ground until they find a tree trunk, then their rhizomes grow little suckers and climb the tree. Only when they reach the canopy do they produce spores. Others twine around stems or scramble over shrubs. A few very slender ferns can even twist their way up the spiny trunks of rattans and palm trees.

A coral fern from Australia. Many fern fronds are divided into small leaflets, which in turn bear even smaller leaflets.

Ant Ferns

A few ferns form special partnerships with ants. As the fern grows old, the center of the rhizome dries out and becomes hollow. Ants move in and set up home there, seeking shelter to rear their young out of sight of predators. The droppings of the ants and their larvae rot, providing the fern with nitrogen compounds. The ants also guard the fern against insects that might try to eat it, biting and stinging the other insects until they go away.

The potato fern of Costa Rica and South America is an ant fern: its large swollen rhizome is full of ants. Local people cook and eat its swollen stems, but first they get rid of the ants.

Check these out:

● Ant ● Climber ● Epiphyte ● Evolution of the Rain Forest ● Plant

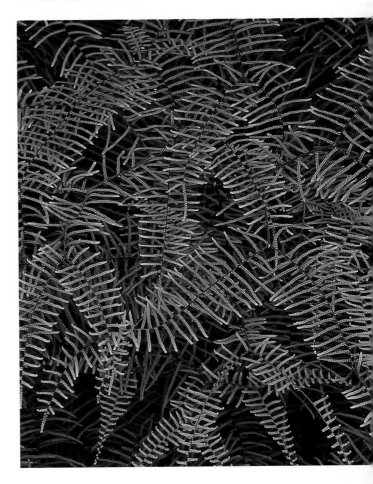

Fish

The great rivers that wind through the world's rain forests are home to hundreds of different kinds of fish. Others live in the millions of small streams that feed the rivers or in oxbow lakes—crescent-shaped lakes that form when river bends get cut off from the main stream by silt. Along river estuaries and coasts, saltwater fish live in swampy mangrove forests.

Tropical fish have a wide range of diets. Some, like the famous piranhas, are fierce killers; others feed on water plants, worms, tiny insects and crustaceans, or even seeds and fruit.

KEY FACTS

●Mudskippers can walk or skip over the mud in mangrove swamps and estuaries along the tropical coasts of the Indian and Pacific Oceans.

●African elephant fish have the largest brains of any fish their size; their brains help them analyze electrical information.

●Lungfish can survive for up to four years in dry mud, waiting for the water to return.

Life in the Dark

Many of the slow-flowing rain forest rivers are muddy, and visibility is poor. Shimmering stripes of glowing red and turquoise run along the sides of the Amazon's neon tetras, helping them recognize each other in murky water.

Most fish have to use other senses instead of sight to find their way around. Some fish that feed on the muddy beds of lakes and rivers grow special fleshy feelers, called barbels, on their snout or chin, that are sensitive to smell and

The iridescent stripes on this neon tetra help other members of its school recognize it in the muddy water of the Amazon River and its tributaries. Tetras' bright colors make them popular aquarium fish.

IN FOCUS

The Water-Monkey

The arowhana, which lives in the floodplains of the Amazon, is sometimes called the water-monkey because it can leap out of the water to seize animals from branches up to 3 ft. (1 m) above the surface. The arowhana can catch animals as large as baby sloths. It has two-part eyes that can focus in the water and above the surface at the same time. It can spot a falling insect or spider before it hits the water.

touch. Long, thin barbels resembling cat's whiskers give catfish their name.

All fish have a lateral line system—a series of pores along their sides and head that lead to a tube lined with sense organs. These detect vibrations in the water caused by other fish, or by water flowing around objects such as rocks.

Large and Small

The arapaima is one of the world's largest freshwater fish. It has been reported to be anywhere between 8 and 15 feet (2.4 and 4.5 m) long and weigh from 220 to 440 pounds (100 to 200 kg), yet it feeds mainly on shrimp and other small water creatures. The arapaima is famous for leaping all the way out of the water to avoid capture.

Size can be deceptive. Piranhas of the Amazonian floodplain are not very big, at most about one foot (30 cm) long, but they can kill animals much larger than themselves by their sheer numbers. Up to 100 piranhas may attack together, swarming around their prey. They tear it to pieces with their short but very sharp teeth, which interlock to prevent the prey's escape. Despite their bad reputation, piranhas usually feed on wounded animals rather than healthy ones. They are also scavengers.

In large river estuaries up to 180 miles (300 km) inland and in mangrove swamps, even more powerful, migrating killers roam. Bull sharks, found in Central and South American rain forests, grow up to 10 feet (3 m) long. They have several rows of teeth in their jaws; as the front ones wear down, the back ones move forward. Sawfish, found in all tropical waters, grow up to 20 feet (6 m) long. Their long narrow snouts have sharp teeth that stick out sideways so they can slash at their prey. They also use their saw-snouts to dig in the mud for shellfish.

The tiniest predator in Amazonian waters is a little blood-red catfish, less than half an inch (1 cm) long. It uses its barbels to find invertebrates in the damp leaf litter of the rain forest. The catfish are left there when floodwaters recede every year.

Sneaky Hunters

Leaf fish are found in South America, Africa, and Asia. A leaf fish looks like a dead leaf, with a dark stripe down the middle like a leaf midrib and a narrow tapering snout like a leafstalk. Leaf fish hide in crevices, like leaves that have become trapped, until small fish come within reach, then they dart out and seize them.

Electric rays—flat fish with long, whiplike tails—lie hidden in the sand in the shallow waters of tropical and mangrove forests all over the world. They stun their prey with electrical discharges of up to six volts. The swordtail characin is not so patient. With a fleshy, red, wormlike lure on its gill cover, it lures prey closer. The wiggling lure draws small fish within reach of the characin's jaws.

Escape Tactics

Some fish have evolved novel ways of avoiding capture. The electric eel of South America stuns or even kills its attackers with an astonishing electric shock, 300 to 600 volts strong.

To escape detection, many fish use camouflage, colors that blend with their backgrounds. Fish that live among waterweeds may have vertical stripes. The pale bellies of other fish hide their shadows, as the shadow of a fish's belly can help a predator to recognize it. The glass catfish of Indonesian rain forest waters is almost completely transparent; the background can be seen through the fish's body.

Life at the Top

Some fish hunt right at the surface of the water. They may pick up insects that have

Mouthfuls of Babies

IN FOCUS

The females of some African cichlids take their eggs into their mouth to keep them safe. Once the babies hatch, they follow their mother around. If danger threatens, they all dash back into her mouth again.

fallen into the water, or they may leap out of the water in pursuit. The archerfish lives in the mangrove swamps of Southeast Asia. By pressing its tongue against a groove in the roof of its pouting mouth, it can shoot a jet of water droplets at insects sitting on a leaf hanging over the water, knocking them down to within its reach.

Guppies also have pouting mouths and often feed at the water surface. The four-eyed fish of Central America and Mexico is a kind of guppy. Its two large bulging eyes sit on the top of its head, like a frog's. It hunts at the water's surface with its eyes half in and half out of the water. Each eye is divided into an upper part and a lower part. The lens can focus two different images at the same time—one from above the water and one from below.

An unusual form of camouflage—the shape of this glass catfish is masked by the background that shows through its transparent body.

the air, it flaps its fins so fast that they make a buzzing sound.

The splashing tetra of South America lays its eggs on leaves overhanging the water, out of the reach of fish that might eat them. The female leaps up and sticks a few eggs on a leaf, then falls back into the water. The male then leaps up and fertilizes them. They repeat the performance until there are about 200 fertilized eggs on the leaf. The male stays behind to splash water over the eggs until they hatch about three days later.

Fish That Walk

Mudskippers live in the mangrove swamps around the Indian and Pacific Oceans. They walk or skip over the mud and up and down the mangrove roots using stiffened fins like little legs. The bases of their belly fins have suckers to help them grip as they climb up the mangroves. From time to time they fill their gill chambers with water from nearby pools so that they can keep breathing. They often sit panting with their mouths open, absorbing oxygen through the lining of their mouth and through their skin.

Breathing Air

The shallow, swampy waters of tropical forest lakes and marshes contain very little dissolved oxygen for fish to use. As the vegetation in the water decays, it uses up oxygen. Some fish have evolved ways of breathing air instead. The walking catfish uses long, lunglike air sacs attached to its gill chamber. Other catfish use their swim bladders as lungs or gulp air into their guts and absorb oxygen from there. The gas-filled swim bladder is used to help the fish float or sink by secreting or absorbing gas from it. Swamp eels and some electric

An archerfish fires a jet of water at an insect on an overhanging leaf. This knocks the insect into the water, where the fish can catch it.

Flying Fish

The butterfly fish of African rain forest waters uses long, winglike fins to fly. It feeds mainly on floating insects but may take to the air in pursuit of an insect or to escape from a predator.

The hatchet fish of South America can fly for several yards, sometimes rising over 3 feet (1 m) above the water. To stay in

An African lungfish lies in a protective mucous cocoon in the mud during the dry season.

eels can take in oxygen through special linings in their mouths.

The most famous air breathers are the lungfish. The Australian lungfish is covered in large scales and has strange lobed fins. Up to 5 feet (1.5 m) long, this big fish still has well-developed gills but can gulp air at the water's surface through its mouth and down its throat. It can obtain sufficient oxygen from the water without rising to the surface to breathe, unless conditions become stagnant. However, its single lung cannot cope with real drought.

The eel-like South American and African lungfish have less-developed gills and use an actual pair of lungs to breathe air. As lakes and pools dry out, lungfish stick their head out of the mud to take a gulp of air. When its pool completely dries up, a lungfish will burrow into the mud, secrete a cocoon around itself, and sleep until water arrives again, breathing through a hole that leads to the mud surface. It can survive like this for up to four years, feeding off its own tissues and losing perhaps half its body weight.

Mating Migrations

Most fish lay eggs. The female sheds her eggs, then the male fertilizes them. This is called spawning. A few fish, such as guppies, actually mate, and the eggs are fertilized inside the female's body. She later gives birth to tiny, fully formed fish.

Many fish, even in the Tropics, breed at particular times of year. The great tropical rivers flood in certain seasons. The floods spread through the forest, and the fish move in to spawn. The flooded forests provide plenty of food for the young fish, and they can hide from predators among the submerged roots and branches. Other fish migrate to small streams with gravelly beds; the eggs sink into the gravel, out of sight of hungry fish.

Check these out:
- Eel ● Fishing ● Flooding
- Mudskipper ● Piranha ● Pirarucu
- River ● Vertebrate ● Water

Fishing

Fishing is a major part of the life of every rain forest community throughout the world. The fish provide a large proportion of the animal protein in their diet.

Amazonian Fishing

The Amazon rain forests are home to caboclos (kuh-BAW-klooz), mixed-race settlers who live on the banks of the Amazon and its many tributaries. They have adopted many of the fishing techniques used for centuries by local peoples.

Seasonal changes in the rivers strongly influence the lives of the caboclos. In the dry season when river levels are low, these fishers rely on their meager agriculture. Their homes are built either on floating rafts or on stilts. Water levels rise tremendously during the wet season, when they spend much of their time fishing since the land they grow their crops on is under many feet of water. They use strong lines and hooks to catch their prey; the lure is often a piece of brightly colored fabric. They also use casting nets, or *tarrafas* (tah-HAH-faws), that they hurl with great skill from the front of their dugouts. They hunt some larger, sedentary or bottom-living species with barbed spears.

At certain times of the year, the caboclos rely on nature to provide a glut of fish.

The *friagem* (free-aw-ZIN) is a phenomenon that sometimes occurs in June. Cold winds blow northward from the cooler southern part of South America. The winds cool down the surface of the river, decreasing the water temperature. This cold water sinks to the bottom, and the oxygen-poor water from the depths floats up to replace it. The fish begin to gasp at the surface for oxygen and are easy pickings for the fishermen.

The Tikuna people, who inhabit the far west of the Amazon River basin on the Brazil-Colombia border, catch fish by poisoning the water. They dig up the roots of a liana (lee-AH-nuh), where one of the plant's long tendrils has reached the soil, and cut it up into 12-inch (30-cm)

A caboclo man from Guyana hurls a fine casting net in the hope of trapping some fish. He may do this several hundred times a day.

215

lengths. Using a wooden mallet, they then crush these against the buttress roots of a tree, wrapping the resulting mash in banana leaves to make a small parcel. The Tikuna then dam a small stream and walk upriver, swishing the packet in the water and releasing clouds of a milky substance as they go. The released chemicals temporarily stun the fish, allowing the Tikuna time to collect them. Those fish that are missed soon recover. Cooking appears to remove all trace of the poison.

Spearing Fish

On some of the smaller islands of the Philippines, local people supplement their diet with food from the rivers that flow through the islands' rain forests. Armed with a rubber catapult and a handful of wooden skewers, they don a pair of plastic goggles and dive into the water. With great precision, they take aim and shoot at small fish and larger river prawns. They emerge with a collection of fish and

Bottom-living and larger fish are hunted by bow and arrow or by spear in Guyana.

Trading in Fish

Collecting live fish for the pet trade has had an impact in the forests of South America and, to a smaller extent, central Africa. In Brazil large numbers of fish are caught and shipped worldwide every year. Most of the species are small, such as tetras, danios, and sometimes angelfish. However, the young of larger species, such as red-tailed catfish, shovel-nosed catfish, and the arowhana, are also exported. As adults these larger fish are all exploited for food. It's not known what effect the removal of these fish has on the environment, but there could be serious consequences if the trade continues unregulated.

crustaceans, each neatly speared on its own wooden skewer, ready for cooking.

Fish Traps

In Sierra Leone, in the upper Guinea rain forest, the Mende people make fish traps out of palm leaves. These stand about 3 feet (1 m) high, are 16 inches (40 cm) in circumference across the top, and taper down to form a cone. The trap is laid on its side on the bed of a small river. Inside, the cone is divided into two chambers, with a small central hole in the middle. Bait, in the form of cooked rice, is placed in the point of the cone. Fish, attracted to the food, swim in through the small hole and cannot escape before the trap is pulled out of the water.

Check these out:

⬤ Eel   Fish   ⬤ Flooding   ◯ Mudskipper
People of the Rain Forest   ⬤ Piranha
⬤ Pirarucu   River   ◯ Water

Flooding

Many of the world's largest tropical rain forests lie on the rich floodplains of the great rivers, such as the Amazon and Orinoco in South America and the Indus and Brahmaputra in India. Large parts of these areas flood each year as a result of seasonal rains falling on mountains far away.

Effects on Plants

The floods bring rich silt that boosts plant growth, but they also cause problems for plants. Herbs and shrubs of the forest floor may be underwater for months. The low light levels underwater slow up photosynthesis, so the plants cannot make much food for themselves.

The oxbow lakes left behind when the rivers change course also become flooded. Plants that float at the surface of these lakes but have roots in the lake bed, such as water lilies, need to grow rapidly to keep up with the rising water. Some grow nearly 10 feet (3 m) a month. The giant water lily of the Amazon can reach the surface 16 feet (5 m) above.

When the floods recede, the lakes dry out. Many plants set seed at the end of the flood and produce new seedlings when the area floods again. Others survive as roots and stems under the mud and produce new shoots when the floods return.

Effects on Animals

As the floodwaters rise, the animals of the forest floor flee upward. Ants, spiders, millipedes, centipedes, and even snails and worms climb up the trees to escape. As the floods rise higher, insect-eating fish move in to feast on those that do not escape in time.

The submerged tree trunks and branches trap particles of organic material in the water, and dense communities of algae and other microscopic creatures grow on it.

This aerial photo shows a flooded Brazilian rain forest. Only the topmost twigs of some trees remain above the water.

These are food for many different fish, such as the jaraqui of the Amazon River basin. This fish has huge fleshy lips covered in fine teeth that rasp at the organic films coating the tree bark. This is a kind of recycling process, since the fish releases the nutrients in its droppings for water plants to use.

Many fish migrate to the flooded forests to spawn. The forest provides shelter for the young, plus insects and seeds for them to feed on.

Many trees use water or fish to disperse their seeds. They produce fruits and seeds during the floods, attracting vast numbers of fish. This is especially true in the Amazon and Orinoco River basins, where the floods last a long time.

Flash Floods

During heavy rainfall, forests act like giant sponges, soaking up rainwater. Where forests are cut down, the rain runs into river valleys, swelling the rivers rapidly and forming flash floods. Flash floods are common in tropical regions, which naturally have periods of very heavy rain.

The flooded Amazonian rain forest, called the igapo, covers nearly 39,000 sq. mi. (100,000 km².)

IN FOCUS

The Piranha Tree

The piranha tree of the Amazon rain forest is pollinated by moths, then produces seeds during the floods. When the floods recede, the tree loses its leaves and produces tender new shoots. These are soon black with hordes of moth caterpillars devouring the young leaves. Many of the caterpillars fall into the water and attract large black piranhas that swarm in to feed on them. After the surviving caterpillars have turned into pupae, the tree grows another crop of leaves that is not attacked. The first crop is a sacrifice the tree makes to help the moths that pollinate it.

The disastrous floods in Guatemala in 1999 were due at least in part to deforestation. Severe rains caused rivers to overflow their banks, flooding the already poor and eroded soil. As a result, thousands of people lost their homes, crops were destroyed, and the economy devastated.

Check these out:
- Deforestation
- Fish
- Migration
- River
- Water

Flowering plants of all shapes and sizes dominate the rain forest. The tallest trees and the smallest herbs on the forest floor produce flowers and seeds. The colors of flowers, which can be seen from far off, attract animals, which pollinate them. The eggs deep inside the flowers' ovaries need to be fertilized by male cells from the pollen grains of another plant or they will not develop into ripe seeds and fruits.

The leaves, flowers, fruits, and seeds provide food for millions of animals, from tiny bugs to monkeys. As well as ferrying pollen from one flower to another, animals carry fruits off to eat them, depositing the seeds some distance from the parent plant.

KEY FACTS

● The giant Amazon water lily has leaves that range from 2 to 6½ ft. (60 to 200 cm) across and flowers 15 in. (38 cm) in diameter.

● Certain plants, such as some wild gingers and acacias, produce special nectaries at which ants can feed. In turn the ants defend the plants from herbivores, biting and stinging the animals to drive them away.

● Some trees, such as the cacao, produce their flowers directly on the tree trunk, where there are no leaves to hide them from the light and from pollinators.

Life in the Shade

Plants of the rain forest floor have to cope with very little light. Many, such as wild ginger, bananas, and many arums, have large leaves to absorb as much light

Some rain forest flowers, like this ground ginger, survive where there is very little light available.

The aptly named hot–lips has lip–shaped sepals that surround tiny starlike flowers.

shade. Others rely on smell or even heat to attract pollinators. Arums, such as the cheese plants, have a single, large, flasklike flower part, the spathe, which may be white or brightly colored. This surrounds a pillarlike structure, the spadix, which bears first female flowers and then male flowers in clusters at its base. The spathe gives off a lot of heat. This helps to spread its scent (which to humans usually smells unpleasant).

Insects attracted by the smell or the warmth crawl inside and are trapped by backward-pointing hairs. They crawl over the female flowers, depositing pollen from other arums on them. They may spend several days in there, until eventually the male flowers ripen, the insects become covered in pollen, and the hairs shrivel to let them escape.

Splashes of Color

In the Tropics, trees may flower year-round. Different individuals of the same species may flower at different times of year. From the air, great splashes of color may be visible where individual trees are flowering. The almendro tree of Costa Rica produces over 500,000 flowers in two months; it may have 20,000 open in a single day. Some rain forest trees shed their leaves for a few days, the better to show off their flowers.

In some Asian forests, many different species of trees over vast areas of forest flower one after the other every five or six years, filling the air with scent. The flowering lasts for months. Some trees may produce 4 million flowers each. A single tree can open 650,000 flowers a day, producing many quarts of nectar.

Yet this grand show appears to be for the benefit of some extremely small

as possible. Some plants manage without light: they feed on rotting leaves. Such plants are usually colorless and have tiny leaves, putting all their energy into producing flowers and fruits. The Malayan *thismia* has no stem or leaves, only flowers. The giant bloom of the parasitic plant *rafflesia*, which grows in Borneo and Sumatra, is over 3 feet (1 m) across and appears as if from nowhere in the leaf litter, arising from tiny threads feeding on the roots of forest plants.

Attracting Pollinators

Some flowers of the forest floor and understory, such as wild ginger and the passionflowers, are large and showy, so insects or birds can spot them even in the

IN FOCUS

Giant Lilies

Some of the showiest forest flowers are on the water: lotuses and water lilies flourish in lakes and slow-moving rivers. Largest of all is the giant Amazon water lily (below), whose flowers are 15 in. (38 cm) across. It attracts beetles with a rich perfume. As they feast on little knobs full of sugar and starch, the lily closes up around them, imprisoning them. Then it starts to shed its pollen. By the next morning, the beetles are well coated with pollen, and the flower opens again to let them escape, only to be trapped in another lily.

insects—thrips, just one sixteenth of an inch (2 mm) long, light enough to drift on the air currents. The thrips come to feed on the petals and pollen. The pollen is covered in oil and sticks to the thrips. These tiny insects stay inside the flowers until the flowers fall to the ground. Then the thrips fly up into the air again. They can produce a new generation of young every eight days, keeping pace with the flowering season.

Showers of Flowers

Many species of rain forest plants can be pollinated only by a particular species of insect, bird, or bat. Insect-pollinated flowers are often pink or blue. Large red, yellow, or orange flowers are often bird pollinated, as birds see these as the brightest flowers. Flowers pollinated by hummingbirds, such as the hibiscus, have down-swept, trumpet-shaped flowers. The bird hovers in front of the flower, and inserts its slender beak and long, thin tongue into the flower to sip nectar. While the hibiscus has large showy flowers, the wild ginger has smaller flowers in a large flower head (inflorescence), which has the same visual impact as a single large flower.

Some liana (climber) flowers are literally little cups of nectar. When they are ripe, they change color from green to yellow then red. Monkeys work their way along the spikes of flowers, lapping up the nectar.

Flowers pollinated by bats need space around them for the bats to navigate. *Parkia* trees of African rain forests produce their flowers above the forest canopy. The flowers look like stubby sausages covered in furry stamens. Many lianas, too, produce clusters of flowers on dangling stems, hanging below the branch, where

221

A relative of the wild ginger, Alpinia *produces clusters of showy flowers on stems several feet tall.*

bats can easily find and reach them. Other bat-pollinated flowers are trumpet-shaped. As the bat thrusts its head into the narrowing flower, it pushes past the pollen-laden stamens. Bat-pollinated flowers open at night and smell like sour milk or sweaty feet, as these are the aromas that attract bats.

Fragrant Oils

Not all insects visit flowers for their nectar or pollen. In tropical America certain orchids lure euglossine bees by offering them fragrant oils that the bees use in their courtship. The flower is shaped like a bucket, with a mushroom-shaped object growing from the rim and a large petal nearby for landing on. When the flower opens, it secretes fluid into the bucket, then gives off a heavy, sweet, soapy scent. The bees home in, land on the edge of the bucket, and begin to scrape at its waxy surface. Then they hover while they transfer the oil to special swellings on their hind legs.

Sooner or later, a bee falls into the bucket. There is only one way to escape—through a narrow tunnel. As the bee struggles to get through, the flower glues two pollen sacs firmly to its back. Any bee already carrying pollen sacs from another bucket orchid has them removed on the way into the tunnel. Another orchid, Catasetum, has sensitive trigger filaments that, if touched, catapult a pair of pollen sacs, sticky end first, onto the bee, sometimes knocking it out of the flower.

Check these out:

● Bat ● Bee and Wasp ● Bird ● Evolution of the Rain Forest ● Hummingbird ● Orchid ● Plant ● Pollination

IN FOCUS

Creating a Stink

One of the world's largest flowers, the titan arum of Sumatra, also produces the world's worst stink. It flowers only once, at the end of its 70-year life, then dies. For seven years it stores food made by its huge leaf, 20 ft. (6 m) tall and 15 ft. (4.5 m) across, in an underground stem. Then the enormous flower rises from the forest floor. A deep trumpet several feet high encloses a tall, pillarlike structure about 9 ft. (2.7 m) high that wafts the stink across the forest, attracting tiny sweat bees and perhaps some beetles.

Fly

There are about 119,500 known species of flies, making them the fourth largest insect order (after beetles, butterflies and moths, and bees and wasps). The family of flies that includes our own familiar housefly is common in the rain forest. These flies are unable to chew and swallow solid food; instead they suck up liquid food using their specialized mouthparts. That is why they tend to feed on soft food such as rotting flesh, fruit, and even animal droppings. They can eat more solid food, but first the fly vomits over it, which has the effect of predigesting it. The fly then sucks up the resulting soup. Not a very hygienic process, it can result in the spread of disease from one animal to another.

Flies play an important role as some of nature's garbage recyclers: they lay their eggs on animal remains. When the larvae hatch, they feed on the dead flesh, helping it to decompose. They then crawl out onto the ground, where they pupate and eventually change into the adult phase of the fly. The whole process takes only seven or eight days.

Livestock Pests

The forests of Central and South America are home to the botfly, the common name for a large parasitic fly also called the warble fly. Botflies lay their eggs on the skin of warm-blooded mammals where they know the victim is likely to get bitten by a blood-sucking mosquito. When the mosquito

KEY FACTS

● Sleeping sickness is caused by the tsetse fly of African rain forests.

● Some fly species have parasitic larvae that feed on the host's living flesh.

● One of the largest flies of the tropical rain forest is the pantophthalmid fly of Central and South America. It can reach a length of over 2⅓ in. (6 cm) and fortunately does not bite.

IN FOCUS

A Drowsy Death

The tsetse (TET-see) fly lives in tropical Africa. Its mouthpart forms a fine, pointed tube, like a hypodermic needle, that pierces skin and sucks up blood. It feeds on the blood of mammals, birds, and reptiles. The tsetse carries a disease known as sleeping sickness, caused by a tiny organism that lives inside the fly and moves to its salivary gland. When the tsetse fly bites a victim to suck its blood, the organism enters the victim's body, where it invades the nervous system and causes drowsiness and often death. However, animals that are repeatedly exposed to sleeping sickness may become immune.

The larvae of the New Zealand glowworm cast their bright, sticky threads in the hope of trapping insects.

strikes, the egg adheres to its mouthparts and is transported to its next victim. There, the newly hatched botfly larva can crawl down into the newly made puncture wound, burrow beneath the skin, and lodge in the muscles. Spines covering the larva's body anchor it in place, and it sends a long, snorkel-like breathing tube up to the skin's surface to obtain oxygen. There, the larva grows and develops, feeding on the flesh of its victim. While the larva feeds, it produces a cocktail of antibiotics to keep the wound disease free. However, once it has pupated and then emerged as an adult fly, the remaining hole in the flesh can become infected and can even cause the host to die.

Many of the cattle living in the botfly range have enormous walnut-sized lumps on their flesh. Some monkeys can be observed with these larvae moving around under the skin on their face.

Robber Flies

The robber fly, found in tropical rain forests throughout the world, is often called the hawk of the insect world. An adept hunter with excellent vision, it can spot and swoop to attack any flying insect passing by. The robber fly will attack bees, wasps, dragonflies, and even large beetles; the prey may be larger than the robber fly itself. This fly's proboscis (pruh-BAH-sus) forms a stabbing tool that pierces its prey and injects saliva that breaks down the internal tissues of its victim, allowing the fly to suck out the resulting soup.

Glowing Larvae

In the caves amid the forests of New Zealand lives a fly known as the New Zealand glowworm. The fly itself is relatively dull and looks just like any other gnat. The larvae though are spectacular. They live on the ceilings of caves overhanging water. The larvae spin silken threads covered in sticky droplets that they dangle from the ceiling. Bioluminescent, they emit a yellowish green light that attracts insects emerging from the water below. As the insects fly up to the lights, they become entangled in the sticky threads, and the larvae reel them in like fishers and devour them.

Check these out:
- Cave - Decomposer - Disease
- Insect - Parasite

Food

Rain forests are the richest of all plant environments, so it is hardly surprising that so many of the fruits, nuts, roots, and leaves that provide humans with food originally came from tropical rain forests and their fringes. Some modern crops are similar to rain forest plants in their wild state, while others have been modified by years of breeding and development by growers. Some new plant varieties were bred to survive in drier lands outside a rain forest environment.

Today many tropical plants are associated more with their new homes than with their original ones. A bunch of bananas in a supermarket cart is such a common sight in most parts of the world that we rarely give it a second thought. However, in prehistoric times wild banana "trees" (really giant-sized herbs) were found only in the hot, humid region that lies between India and New Guinea, in the rain forest zone of Southeast Asia.

Humans soon discovered that some banana varieties were good to eat and learned to grow them as crops. From Southeast Asia, banana cultivation spread to eastern and central Africa, perhaps over 2,000 years ago, and eventually to the Americas, the Pacific islands, and finally Australia.

Bananas are not all yellow and sweet. Some ripen to a reddish color; many are green, hard, and starchy. Some large bananas, called plantains, can be eaten cooked, ripe or green.

KEY FACTS

● The fruit of the guava contains a huge amount of vitamin C, which is particularly good for teeth and gums and helps the body resist colds.

● The creamy green avocado is a fruit that tastes more like a vegetable. It contains more protein than any other fruit and is one of the richest foods one can eat.

● The main ingredient of chewing gum, chicle, comes from the tropical sapodilla tree that grows in Central America.

Many varieties of bananas grow in the world's rain forest zones. They are a rich source of nutrients.

The long-established way to squeeze palm oil from the fruit is by trampling it with bare feet. These women are working near Mamfe in Cameroon's southwestern region.

Bananas may seem to be a luxury fruit, but in many parts of the world they remain a staple crop, a basic food that forms an important part of the everyday diet. Harvesting bananas is extremely dangerous—poisonous spiders inhabit banana bunches. They can kill human banana-gatherers.

African Exports
The oil palm is native to the western and central African rain forests, although varieties are now also grown in Southeast Asia. Widely cultivated in plantations, each year the oil palm produces up to six bunches of about 200 densely packed, individual fruits. The outer layer of the fruit is rich in oil, and so is the inner kernel of the seed, known as the nut. Palm oil is used to make margarine, cooking oil, and nonfoods such as soap. Wild forest palms produce lesser amounts of oil. In western Africa palm oil is used to make an alcoholic drink called palm wine.

Coffee shrubs grow wild in the Congo rain forests as well as in drier

IN FOCUS

A Tropical Chew

The sapodilla tree of the Central American forests has a very tasty, brownish fruit filled with a sweet pulp. However, the tree also provides humans with another product. Since ancient times, the people of Central America have cut its bark to extract a rubbery, milky fluid called latex. This is heated into a sticky gum called chicle, which is still the chief ingredient of chewing gum.

regions in the Horn of Africa and Arabia. They were soon cultivated across eastern Africa, India, and Southeast Asia, and by the 1700s, had been introduced to Central and South America. Two chief varieties are cultivated: arabica and robusta. In Africa and Asia, coffee is now mostly grown in highland areas, since leaf disease is common in the lowlands.

The shrub produces glossy green leaves and white flowers. The small berries, which ripen to red, contain two bitter seeds called beans. Coffee beans are produced by removing the flesh of the berry, soaking the beans in water, and then drying them in the sun. The beans are ground or processed to provide the world with one of its favorite hot beverages.

From Asia and Oceania

For thousands of years, southern Asia was famous for its trade in spices. Many of these spices are now grown in other tropical countries around the world. Nutmeg and mace come from the same Indonesian tree: nutmeg is the seed and mace is its aril, or sheath. The clove is another spice-producing tree from Indonesia, which since the 1800s has been widely grown on Zanzibar and neighboring African islands. After blossoming, the clove calyxes (the cups that hold the growing seed) are beaten from the boughs and dried in the sun. They are used to flavor drinks and food and to make oils used in medicines.

Sri Lankan cinnamon is produced from the bark of a tall tree. Pepper comes from India, where it grows in hot, wet regions. A climbing vine, it produces long clusters of red peppercorns, which may be dried to make black pepper or soaked and stripped of their outer covering to make white

These coffee berries are ripening on the stem in East Java, Indonesia. They contain the bitter seeds, or beans, that will be roasted to make coffee.

pepper. A kind of root called a rhizome, ginger also grows in hot, wet climates. It is boiled, peeled, dried, and then prepared in various forms, such as powder, to flavor foods, candies, and drinks.

Asia produces many fruits in its rain forest zones. The rambutan grows in Malaysia, a tall tree with clusters of spiked red fruit. The white aril that forms around the seed is the part that is eaten. The mangosteen comes from the same part of the world, a large tree with purple fruits containing moist white flesh.

The mango is one of the most popular of all tropical fruits. Native to India and Myanmar, it is now grown in all tropical lands. It grows best on the edges of the

227

rain forest, as it does not thrive in a climate that is rainy throughout the year.

Many citrus fruits such as the orange, rich in vitamin C, originated in southern China and Southeast Asia. Most are now cultivated beyond the rain forest belt, in drier climates. The lime, a native of India, is also a tropical fruit.

The sago palm grows wild in the tropical swamps of Indonesia and Malaysia. It is felled and stripped of its bark to remove the pith inside. This is rich in sweet starch, which is processed to make a kind of flour and for use in desserts.

Sugarcane is a member of the grass family, which originally grew in the hot, humid areas of eastern India and Bangladesh. Now grown in many tropical lands, it is a major crop in the rain forest zones of Central America and northern South America.

Rice is another grass. Tropical strains of rice thrive in rainwater, and many first grew as wild plants in the muddy valleys of rivers that ran through the forests of Southeast Asia. Most rice is still grown in fields flooded by irrigation. Rice is by far the most important food crop in Asia and and is the chief resource for feeding a hungry world. Varieties of rice can now be grown far from the Tropics, even in the warmer parts of Europe.

Breadfruit, another staple crop, is grown on many islands in the Pacific Ocean. A large, round fruit with a rough greenish-brown skin, it is packed with a starchy white pulp that can be cooked. The fruit comes from a tall evergreen tree with glossy leaves that originated in the forests of Malaysia.

A family of climbing plants from across Africa and Asia, yams grow swollen underground stems called tubers. These are full of starch and are a staple crop in many parts of the Tropics.

Cassava (or manioc) is processed at a village in Guyana. This starchy root is grown throughout the Tropics.

Macadamia trees are grown on the Hawaiian Islands and in Australia. The nuts of this tree are rich in fat and are used in making cakes and pastries or eaten on their own; some people consider them the most delicious of all nuts. The trees are native to Queensland, in northern Australia's rain forest belt.

All-American Foods

The tropical regions of Central and South America have produced a vast range of food plants that are now eaten around the world. Cacao is an evergreen tree of the Central and South American rain forest. It has pink blossoms and produces yellow pods that each contain about 100 seeds (called beans), which grow in a white pulp. The beans are dried, roasted, and ground into a powder called cocoa, used to make drinks, candies, and chocolate. Since the

1600s cacao plantations have flourished in the rain forest zones of western and central Africa and in Southeast Asia.

Many candies, ice creams, and puddings—and perfumes too—include vanilla essence. Vanilla is a climbing plant, a type of orchid originally from the Central American forests. It grows a bean pod about 8 inches (20 cm) long, which is harvested when still unripe. This is dried in the sun and left for several months. The seeds are then crushed and treated with alcohol to extract the essence. The rain forest zone of Madagascar is now the primary producer of vanilla.

Fruits of the American Tropics have also been spread far and wide. The flavorful papaya, also known as papaw or pawpaw, is a large yellowish fruit with orange-pink flesh. It grows from a tree-sized herb. The guava is pale yellow when ripe, and it can be stewed or made into a jam or jelly that is popular in the Caribbean. Passion fruit is commonly used to make juice drinks. A relative of the passion fruit, though less widely grown, the giant granadilla bears green or yellow-green fruit that can be boiled to use as a vegetable. Also less common is the custard apple, a family of tropical trees with aromatic leaves, fragrant flowers, and edible fruits.

The most successful fruit of tropical South America is the pineapple, which forms a single large fruit from a mass of separate blossoms. The sweet, rather fibrous fruit grows from a cluster of tough, swordlike leaves. Pineapples were taken to Europe, Africa, and southern Asia in the 1500s and 1600s and to Australia and the Hawaiian Islands in the 1800s.

The avocado, which grows on smallish trees, has a dark green skin and pale green creamy flesh. A native of Central American forests, it is now grown in many tropical areas, including eastern Africa, and in nontropical regions such as the southern United States and Israel.

Capsicum plants include sweet peppers and red peppers. Long red or green chili peppers provide plenty of heat to human taste buds. Natives of the tropical

The large pods of the cacao tree contain the beans used to make chocolate. They grow directly on the tree trunk.

IN FOCUS

Cocoa Cash

The first people to make a frothy chocolate drink were the Aztecs, who lived in Mexico about 500 years ago. They made the drink from cacao beans ground into a powder, boiled, and whisked up with water and honey. Cacao beans from the tropical forest were so valuable that the Aztecs often used them instead of coins to pay for goods in the market.

Americas, capsicums are now grown around the world; hot peppers have become an essential part of much Asian cooking as well as of Latin American and U.S. dishes.

One staple crop of the South American Tropics is cassava, also known as manioc. It has also been grown in Africa and Asia since the 1600s. A shrub, its tuber is rich in starch. The tuber is peeled, then boiled and mashed or grated. It can be used to make a kind of flour and flaked to make a dessert called tapioca. The leaves of the plant are sometimes boiled and eaten too.

Another successful crop from wet, tropical climates is the sweet potato, a starchy tuber that also first came from South America. The plant has rambling green leafy stems, and its purplish tubers are often long and pointed. Although sometimes called a yam, the sweet potato is a different plant from the yams of tropical Africa and Asia.

The peanut, also known as the groundnut, is from the South American Tropics but is now grown in the rain forest zones of western and central Africa and in other climates, such as that of the southern United States. The nuts are seeds that form underground in pods.

Brazil nuts grow on tall trees that grow only in the wild in the Amazon River basin. They are the tough-cased seeds of a large, round fruit. The nuts are large, with a white center rich in protein and fat. A popular food, Brazil nuts are also used in soaps and shampoos.

IN FOCUS

A Sign of Friendship

A relative of the cacao, the kola or cola tree is native to western Africa. Its woody fruits contain a large, dark brown seed called a kola nut. Like coffee and tea, kola is rich in caffeine. This is a stimulant, something that keeps people awake. Although it tastes very bitter, the nut is chewed for its caffeine content. Throughout western Africa, a kola nut is a gift that signifies friendship and hospitality. Kola essence has also been used to flavor soft drinks of the types called colas, although artificial flavoring is now normally used instead.

A Wild Food Bank

Wild strains of many tropical food crops still grow in the rain forests. These may not produce the high yields of cultivated plants, but it is crucial that they be preserved. Wild plants have genes that may be valuable to growers; for example, they may prove to be resistant to certain plant diseases. And it is always likely that the world's rain forests may still have many valuable food plants that so far have remained undiscovered.

Check these out:

● **Biotechnology** ● **Fruit** ● **Herb and Spice**

Food Web

There are two ways to visualize how animals and plants interact in an ecosystem: as a food chain and as a food web. A food chain traces a single chain of eating and being eaten, from caterpillar to bird to wild cat, for example. A food web traces all the food chains in a habitat, such as the rain forest, and all the links between them. For example, the leaves of a hibiscus tree may be eaten by caterpillars, sloths, and leaf-cutter ants. These in turn may be eaten by many predators of different sizes, which in turn may fall prey to even larger predators; the larger predators may eat many kinds of animals.

KEY FACTS

● In a food web, plants are known as producers and animals are known as consumers.

● Big hunters, such as the tiger and leopard, are at the top of the food web, with no other natural predators besides humans.

● Chimpanzees are omnivores: they eat more than 90 different species of plants and catch over 20 different kinds of prey.

At the base of the food web are the plants. Unlike animals, plants can produce new living material from simple minerals and water taken up from the soil, together with carbon dioxide gas from the atmosphere, using the energy of sunlight. For this reason plants are called producers.

All animals eat either plants or other animals that have eaten plants, or a little of both. Animals are called consumers. They use food to provide the building blocks for their own bodies and the energy for moving, keeping warm, mating, and, of course, eating. In this way the energy from sunlight trapped by plants powers all life in the rain forest.

Some of the smallest predators in the Trinidad rain forest, army ants attack a beetle larva. Lots of ants work together to kill the much larger animal.

231

Herbivores, Carnivores, and Omnivores

Animals that eat plants are called herbivores. Plant material is surprisingly tough. Plant cell walls contain cellulose, which is difficult to digest. In fact, a lot of the consumed plant material remains undigested and passes out in droppings. Herbivores produce more droppings for their size than any other animals. This means they do not extract all the energy from their food. Herbivores therefore need to eat a lot of food to get enough nutrients.

Carnivores are flesh eaters, feeding on prey they have just killed—fresh meat. They can afford to spend a lot of energy chasing prey, then have a large meal and rest up for a while. Most plant eaters, on the other hand, need to keep eating all day. Meat eaters, too, waste some of their food: very few can digest bones, fur, or feathers.

Hunting is not a reliable way of getting food—the hunter may not catch anything for some time, so carnivores can usually go quite a long time without eating. They live off their fat until the next successful hunt. Large pythons may not eat for months after swallowing a big mammal.

There are not as many carnivores as herbivores; if there were, the carnivores would soon run out of prey. However, carnivores hunt at every level of the rain forest. The forest rivers and lakes, too, have their carnivores, from fierce underwater insect larvae to river dolphins, crocodiles, and caimans.

Some animals are both herbivores and carnivores, called omnivores. Chimpanzees, monkeys, wild hogs, peccaries, bears, foxes, and raccoons are omnivores. They will feed on leaves, flowers, fruits, and mushrooms, as well as on smaller animals, including dead ones. Bears, for example, will feed on fruit and steal kills from big cats, but they will also kill for themselves if hungry.

A RAIN FOREST FOOD WEB

Energy trapped by plants (producers) is passed on to animals (consumers) when they eat plants, and to other animals that eat the first animals. At each stage energy is lost in droppings (undigested food) and as heat given off by the many chemical reactions in the bodies of plants and animals, so the mass of the top consumers is much less than the mass of the plants.

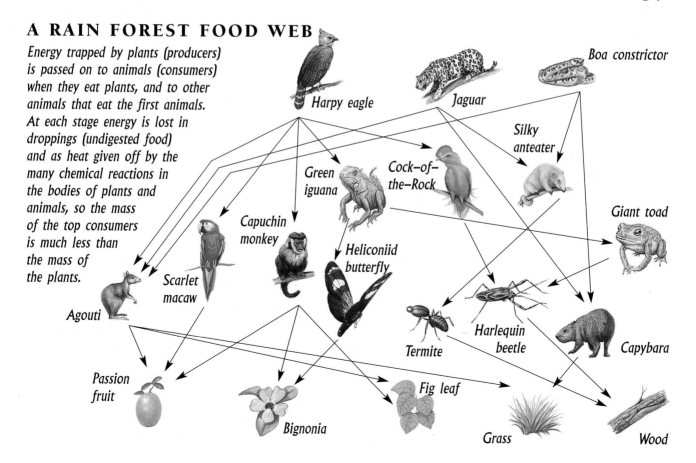

Harpy eagle · Jaguar · Boa constrictor · Silky anteater · Green iguana · Cock-of-the-Rock · Giant toad · Capuchin monkey · Scarlet macaw · Heliconiid butterfly · Agouti · Termite · Harlequin beetle · Capybara · Passion fruit · Bignonia · Fig leaf · Grass · Wood

Scavengers

Scavengers feed on dead animals, but many also consume fallen fruits. In many rain forests the most important scavengers are the ants. They may be small, but they are present in astronomical numbers. Ants will work as a team to drag dead animals and leaves much larger than themselves to their nests to eat. In some forests land crabs take over this role, using their pincers to tear up the remains of animals and plants. Slugs, snails, and cockroaches are everywhere, from the forest floor to the highest canopy. Earthworms eat their way through the soil itself, extracting any dead organic material and excreting the rest as worm casts.

Lured by the scent and sight of meat, flies home in to feed and lay their eggs. Working their way out from the inside, fly maggots can reduce a mouse corpse to a skeleton in just a few days.

Decomposers

Decomposers are some of the most important organisms in the forest. Without them, piles of dead leaves, fallen logs, and corpses would build up and make the forest a nasty, smelly place. Decomposers feed on what is left of dead plants and animals after the scavengers have had their fill. They break the remains down to chemicals that are released into the soil and can be taken up again by plants. Without decomposers the soil would soon run out of nutrients.

The most important decomposers are fungi and bacteria. They feed by secreting digestive juices onto plant and animal remains, then absorbing the digested food. Beneath the leaves on the forest floor is a vast network of fungal threads working away on the remains that lie there.

IN FOCUS

Keystone Species

There are very few top carnivores in rain forests (like this jaguar feeding on a turtle), since they need many smaller animals to feed on. Therefore, the health of a forest can be measured by its population of top carnivores. If the forest is being damaged by logging, pollution, or disturbance by people, these are the first animals to disappear. If conservation programs were designed to protect these keystone species, the whole habitat, including many other animals and plants, would be saved.

Check these out:

- Carnivore
- Decomposer
- Feeding
- Fungus
- Herbivore
- Insectivore

Glossary

Algae: plantlike organisms that produce their own food by photosynthesis but do not have proper stems, leaves, and veins.

Anesthetic: a chemical that numbs the tissues so that an animal feels no pain.

Archaeologist: someone who excavates ancient remains and studies them scientifically.

Aril: a covering or sheath found on certain seeds.

Bacteria: simple microscopic single-celled creatures.

Biodiversity: the variety of plant and animal life.

Bioluminescent: the ability of an animal to produce light as the result of a chemical reaction within its body.

Bromeliad: any of over 1,000 plants of the pineapple family. Most bromeliads grow as epiphytes.

Bush meat: the flesh of wild animals killed for food.

Caboclo: a mixed-race riverside settler in Amazonia, descended from European (mainly Portuguese) settlers and the local Indian population.

Chitin: a very hard hornlike substance that forms the external skeleton of insects, spiders, and crustaceans and is present in the cell walls of fungi.

Compost: rotting vegetation that has reached a finely divided state.

Cretaceous: the period of geological time from about 144 to 65 million years ago, during which the dinosaurs dominated Earth and mammals and flowering plants spread across the land.

Deciduous: pertaining to trees that lose their leaves in winter.

Ecological niche: the part of the environment in which an animal is adapted to live.

Estuary: a water passage where a river meets the sea.

Excretion: something that has been pushed out or has seeped out.

Extinction: the final dying out of an animal or plant species.

Fossil: the remains of an animal, usually only the bones, preserved with minerals and turned to rock.

Incubate: the development and hatching process of eggs in the presence of heat.

Insoluble: something that cannot be dissolved in water.

Invertebrate: an animal that lacks a spinal column (backbone).

Larva: the early stage of an insect's life that may look completely different from the adult.

Liana: a climbing plant with long tendrils that grows up trees to support itself and reach sunlight.

Mangrove: one of various trees and shrubs that grow along muddy coasts and river estuaries.

Microorganism: an organism (living creature) too small to see without the aid of a microscope.

Nectar: sweet, sugary liquid produced by flowers to attract the insects and animals that will pollinate them.

Neotropical: species that live in the Tropics of the New World (the Americas).

Nutrient: any substance used as food by living things.

Pharmaceutical: used in the preparation of medicines.

Pistil: the part of a flower to which pollen grains stick.

Poacher: someone who illegally catches, kills, or collects animals or plants.

Pollen: the powderlike spores that carry the male sex cells to the female parts of another flower.

Prehensile: able to grasp things like a hand.

Pupa: the stage in an insect's life cycle when the tissues of the larva (grub or caterpillar) are replaced by those of the adult. Pupae are usually encased in a hard covering or a silk cocoon.

Rehabilitation: the care of an injured animal, with the ultimate aim of releasing it back into the wild.

Rhizome: creeping underground stem, often swollen with stored food.

Scavenger: an animal that feeds on dead and decaying plant or animal matter.

Silt: very fine mud whose rock particles are 1/20 millimeter or less in diameter.

Spore: a minute, dustlike reproductive cell produced by mosses, liverworts, ferns, and fungi.

Stamen: the male part of a flower.

Starch: a tasteless white carbohydrate found in rice, wheat, seeds, tubers, and other parts of plants.

Temperate Zone: the part of Earth between the Tropics and the polar circles.

Tropics: the regions on either side of the equator that remain warm throughout the year.

Tundra: a flat area of the Arctic where the soil is permanently frozen.

Understory: the layer of trees and shrubs between the forest floor and the canopy.

Index